M000076485

OF CABBAGES AND KINGS

A COLLECTION OF TRUE SHORT STORIES
THAT CELEBRATE
THE GOOD, BAD, UGLY & FUNNY THINGS
THAT MAKE LIFE WORTH LIVING

RANDA M. CHANCE

Copyright © 2013 Randa M. Chance

All rights reserved

ISBN: 0988785307
ISBN-13: 978-0-9887853-0-4

For Donna Hieftje,
who always knew

PREFACE

"...And then there are those other days, those desolate days when everything is wrong and my foundations are shaking. When dark, thick sadness threatens to overwhelm me and my soul is bruised. That is when I pull out a memory like one of these. I hold it in my calloused hands and turn it over and over and hold it up to the light. I examine it from every angle and relive it again."
--Randa Chance, Of Cabbages and Kings

Do you think an experience needs to be big and important to be valuable? What about those small, funny, poignant moments, those that don't seem to be very significant? Can you actually learn life lessons from those simple things in life?

Randa Chance shares true-life stories that are gut-wrenchingly sad, side-splittingly hilarious, and achingly tender. Laugh out loud with her as she swallows a bobby pin and when she becomes psychotic at the end of her pregnancy. Sigh with her when she meets her remarkable husband. Cry along with her as she realizes that, as a young mother, and the wife of a church-planting pastor husband, there's no food to feed their kids, nor money to buy any. Each vignette charms the reader with real emotions and you'll keep turning the pages to read "just one more."

Randa Chance shows readers from all walks of life that significant moments don't have to be big and important to truly matter. Sometimes a moment consists of a fully-clothed grandmother executing a cannonball dive into the creek, just to help her family say good-bye with smiles instead of tears. Sometimes it's about finding the funny in the insensitive, instead of taking offense. Sometimes a moment is about how Christmas can still be special – even after you burn down the house. Randa manages to find those priceless moments while juggling life as a wife, mother, pastor's wife and a writer.

Readers from all walks of life will be challenged to hold those they love just a little closer, to consciously appreciate not just the big moments but also the little ones, and to find contentment, laughter and beauty even in some of life's most difficult circumstances.

--Karen Gordon Hemmes

FOREWORDS

Randa Chance has a way of storytelling like no other. She has that rare give of recounting everyday moments that, without warning, squeeze your heart until you surrender to the sweet struck wonder of its tears and its laughter.

Randa speaks into our heart with a depth of wisdom and wealth of knowledge and understanding, but she has been able to bring it down to the place we live. She serves up the art of living in royal 24-karat bowls of word pictures, filling them with ordinary but delicious humor, and sometimes tearful sighs of remembrance for those days gone by which were simple and uncomplicated. She is in her own class and I am confident that we will see much acclaim about her brilliant writing in the years to come.

--Nancy J. Grandquist, Author,
Songwriter and Recording Artist

This morning I sat down to do a quick overview of this book. However, after the first few words I knew I was hooked and would not stop until I reached "The End". While reading I found myself smiling, sniffling, crying, smiling, chuckling, and experiencing the rare but great fun of when chuckling erupted into laugh-out-loud moments as you skillfully drew me, the reader, into your stories. Randa, I rarely have such a gift of spontaneous belly laughs. Thank you!

I clearly remember the cool of the restaurant, the burning heat outside, with friends sitting at the table, relaxing during the busyness of a conference and you, possibly a little self-consciously, mentioning you wanted to write a book. I looked at you and knew that one day you would do just that, and I also knew it would be an amazing book. I carefully marked my calendar and set up reminders to pray for this project. Time went by but I never doubted that this book, Of Cabbages and Kings, would become a reality. And I was right -- it is an amazing book.

Thank you, Randa, for sharing your real life stories filled with honest insights about the things that really matter — love, life, and laughter. You take the ordinary moments of life and help us see the sacred. Whether your stories were based on parenting children, planting churches, or facing personal challenges, ranging from the hilarious to the heartbreaking, your honest love for God, Shane, your precious children, and people (of all kinds) came shining through.

--Rev. Cindy Miller, Ph.D. (ABD)

ACKNOWLEDGEMENTS

I always dreamed about what that "published author" picture would look like on my first book. I wanted it to convey the spirit and atmosphere in which I penned my heartrending stories and brought the reader to tears and laughter.

In my mind's eye was a soft-edged scene of myself as a skinny, dreamy-eyed girl in a dark, silent room, seated at a beautifully scrolled and distressed antique desk, writing stories by hand on unlined paper. This picture was, naturally, in sepia tones, and a gentle sort of light always shone down on my head through a glass window.

Recently I realized that I was also delusional.

What I had concocted was an idealized image that combined Jo from Little Women with Anne of Green Gables. I am far from resembling either one of those fictional creatures.

In reality, skinny went out the window about the time I got married, and being the wife of a pastor, mother of three children, and working a full-time job outside the home does not lend itself to a great deal of alone time. This manuscript was mostly written in those rare snatches of quiet in the wee hours of morning with a laptop that was missing many keys, when my eyes were gritty and bloodshot and my hair was sticking up all over my head.

The only time I wrote one of these stories by hand was when I forgot my laptop in my haste to catch a plane, and had to chicken-scratch on a legal pad for hours. When I tried to transcribe my own notes a few days later, I could barely decipher my left-handed hieroglyphics.

My deepest thanks to the following individuals, without whom this book would not exist:

Harry Fleming (designedbyharry.com) for your brilliant cover design and understanding of the concept. The world is a much better looking place because of you.

Brandy Steele (Brandy Steele Photography), my cousin and photographer extraordinaire who had some incredible ideas for the jacket photo and came up with what you see. (It also looks a thousand times better than my typical frazzled-housewife-at-midnight getup.)

Karen Gordon Hemmes, my fellow curly-headed friend, for assembling a magnificent book jacket teaser.

Krystal Mayville and Keli Schlueter, my sisters, who tweaked the things that needed to be, and read and edited and laughed at me and provided blunt, no-nonsense feedback that hurt and challenged.

Donna Hieltje, my brown-eyed teacher-mentor who discovered and coaxed out the writer in me so many years ago.

Randy and Mary Mayville, my parents, who read and laughed and cried and encouraged, and said, "On your next book cover, you need to put Gage and Benjamin's faces in front of each cabbage, and stick Devon's head under that crown."

Shane, Devon, Gage and Benjamin, my own little clan, I love you for putting up with me, and for the immeasurable joy and happiness you have brought. You are my life.

Jesus, my best friend, who gave me the strength to finish writing this when I did not think it ever would be possible.

CONTENTS

Introduction 15

The Change..16

Why Some Animal Mothers Eat Their Young 19

Devon and Mimi......................................23

The Hard Parts 32

The Great Toilet Caper 45

Let Me Hold You 64

Stalled Out...69

The Preacher's Seat 74

The Demon Ball......................................81

Planting a New Baby 87

The Others...96

Bobby Pins, Bees and Other Creatures...............106

Trials by Fire 122

Love...135

Nanny's Hands.......................................145

The Boxers..148

The Plagues...159

Any Given Sunday 177

One Wild Nativity....................................185

The Night Everything Changed 205

Uncertain Identity 216

Amazing Grace.......................................221

The Formaldehyde Baby 236

Thankful...245

"...The time has come," the Walrus said,
"To talk of many things:
Of shoes--and ships--and sealing-wax--
Of cabbages--and kings--
And why the sea is boiling hot--
And whether pigs have wings."... .

Excerpted from
"The Walrus and The Carpenter"
Lewis Carroll

(from *Through the Looking-Glass and
What Alice Found There*, 1872)
(Public Domain)

INTRODUCTION

Dear Reader,

This little book is composed of many true stories, some long, some short.

Some are huge and life-shattering, and some are little vignettes of moments, but they all had an impact. Some are cabbages, and some are kings.

And they are all important. They teach us to be grateful for this good gift of life that comes from above.

One small heart beating with thankfulness can grow into a strong foundation of peace and stability and contentment.

So be thankful. Love deeply. Be content. Laugh at yourself. Allow tears to fall. And treasure the journey traveled.

THE CHANGE

It's a whirlwind that sucks you up into the heights of happiness and drops you on your head at the most unexpected moments. It fills you with dread of the unknown and breathless anticipation.

You find yourself throwing your head back and roaring with laughter one second, and sniffling back unshed tears the next. It could be described as insanity or bipolar disorder, but it's not. It's just being a parent.

If you've been there, you're nodding. If you're not there yet, buckle up and hang on.

It changes your life. It shatters your ideals. It overturns quiet, pristine homes into a hodgepodge of smudged mirrors, science projects in the closets, thundering stairs and happy shrieks.

Designer purses turn into diaper bags that smell like crayons and Cheez-Its. Golf clubs and mature fireside conversations with expensive coffee in hand fade to messy toy rooms, sticky faces and the occasional baby bottle found under the couch, half-full of milk that has started to sprout.

Lazy, slept-in mornings take a number until retirement, because every Saturday the master bed becomes a trampoline at 6:59 a.m. on the dot.

Laundry becomes one of the greatest trials you will ever face.

You find yourself shoving your meticulous plans for life onto the back burner so that you can plan trips to the zoo.

You gain the ability to give kisses that carry instant magical healing qualities, and when you can't heal, you ache in places that you never knew could hurt.

You melt into a puddle when you receive a handmade love note or a dirty rock that has been picked out especially for you with detailed instructions for its care. You cry when they think they're too old to kiss you goodbye at school. You wish you could watch them grow up in slow motion so you don't miss a single second.

Your heart lives outside of your body, vulnerable in a way you never thought possible. You watch for the changes that let you know they're growing up, and you find immense pleasure in hearing them use words in the wrong context, because it means they're learning.

You find yourself instinctively raising a shoulder when you hold them close and cup their head in your hand, as if that could protect them from the world.

You press your cheek against that tiny head and breathe deep, and you realize it smells nicer than expensive perfume.

You've traded steaks for McDonald's and given up manicures to give bubble baths to chubby little bottoms and create soapy hairdos that defy gravity and bring on hysterical laughter.

Gentleness suddenly becomes you. Bitten tongues hold back words that could damage tender hearts.

And you wouldn't have it any other way. That's what makes it so extraordinary.

These little moments.

WHY SOME ANIMAL MOTHERS
EAT THEIR YOUNG

It was the week before Christmas. Life as we knew it had been turned upside down and we were devastated. We needed a break. On a Sunday evening we went out of town with the kids and took a mini-vacation to Boerne, TX for the night. It was dark and cold. The air was sharp and stung our noses. The little people stomped along in front of us huffing out clouds of steam and exclaiming over their thoughts of Santa Claus.

All down Main Street the holiday lights shimmered and people wandered through tiny shops looking for the perfect present. We walked about for a few minutes, but Devon and Gage were only concerned about finding hot chocolate and donuts and having a picnic next to the river, so there we went.

Gage was mightily impressed with the bright stars and pointed upward with his mouth hanging open.

"Mom, Mom! Look! There's the Big Dip! Ohh, look! The Tiny Dip! It's right over there too!"

He gazed toward the sky as the rotor blades of a helicopter suddenly thumped against the air above us and then the sound was muffled as it faded into the clouds. "Look-a there!" Gage yelled, "It's a wallyhop-ter!"

Beside the river was a tacky sculpture in the shape of a Christmas tree made entirely out of strings of lights. We climbed in between the lights and sat on the ground underneath eating our donuts. The kids looked like little hobbits wrapped in our oversized coats. Gage spilled his hot chocolate and howled his displeasure. We took pictures of the kids twirling in happy, dizzy circles under the lights until they collapsed.

The ducks swimming close to the shore discovered that we had donuts and came quacking. We took our leftovers and stood next to the river in the freezing air throwing crumbs.

Devon was intrigued by the crippled duck with one foot who could barely swim in a circle, and she fed it until it became bored and wobbled down the river.

She turned around and walked back up the hill and began to sing a made-up song to the tune of "Where, Oh Where, Has My Little Dog Gone."

Oh, my lord is big
And my lord is little
Where, oh, where can he be?
Shake your legs and shake your booty
Where, oh, where can he be?

On the midnight ride back home, we wrapped up the kids in blankets and turned the heater on high. They snored in the backseat, their faces covered in remnants of chocolate, strands of sticky hair pasted to their forehead and cheeks. The stars were crystal clear against the night and the trees stood in dark silhouettes as we drove in silence. All was calm. We had found a little time of peace in the midst of our sadness.

The next afternoon as I worked at home, I realized that Gage had become very quiet. I went downstairs to investigate and hollered out in surprise.

A carefully distributed thick layer of whole wheat bread pieces lay before me. It led downward from the steps where I stood, throughout the living room, into the family room, and all over the kitchen floor. The entire carpet downstairs was polka dotted with crumbs.

I marched up behind him where he was pulling the last heel of bread out of a now empty bag and beginning to pull it apart.

"Gage! What are you doing?"

He jumped and turned around.

"Um....."

"What? What possessed you to do such a thing?"

"I'm feedin' dem ducks, Mamma."

I sat down in the middle of the crumbs and laughed until I cried. Gage was puzzled.

I got out the hand vacuum and gave it to him. "Come on, buddy, let's pick these up."

We sucked up bread for the next hour, and then he tore off in search of his next adventure.

DEVON AND MIMI

Mimi was adored. She was my mother-in-law and the grandmother to our children.

Devon and Mimi were very close. They both loved clothes and shopping and things that sparkled. They danced around and giggled together and Devon spent many nights at her house. Mimi would take Devon to the store and Devon would return home ecstatic, loaded down with completely unnecessary toys and miniature designer purses that fit her perfectly. They were quite the pair.

She took Devon shopping for her sixth birthday. I think she knew it was their last shopping trip together. Her birthday budget was $100.00, but when I met her to pick up Devon, it was quite obvious that she had spent more than that.

Devon was full of excitement over her spoils. She exclaimed happily over her favorites, the tiny working sewing machine, her Dooney & Bourke bumblebee purse, and the manicure Mimi had taken her to get.

Mimi slowly hobbled around the truck to get Devon out. She was in pain but would not let me help. Her face was grey and drawn, but she smiled and nuzzled Devon's nose with Eskimo kisses and then hugged her tight. When I tried to ask her if she was feeling okay, she glared at me and mouthed, "Shut up!"

We found out just a few weeks later that the cancer had returned with a vengeance and was spreading through her bones. She adored her children and grandchildren, and she fought the disease with every fiber of her being.

By late spring, the cancer spread to her organs. Mimi was told she had a few months left. We sobbed in our private moments and put on happy faces when we went to see her.

As a family, all of her children and grandchildren began taking turns staying at her house, cleaning, cooking, bringing her popsicles and spending almost every waking minute with her.

The cancer spread to her brain. Mimi hated the thought of not being a part of her grandchildren's lives, so she finally decided to try chemotherapy. It was applied directly to her brain through her spinal cord. It did not work. All of her hair fell out in a matter of hours.

The cancer affected her facial muscles. Her eyelid and cheek began to droop on one side. It was difficult for her to smile and speak normally, but her valiant attempts paid off and she talked just fine. Tiny and bald, she was still beautiful.

In August, she was told she had about six weeks left.

Shane and I finally decided we needed to help Devon prepare to tell Mimi goodbye. She was almost seven years old and surely old enough to have some understanding. We did not want it to be a surprise for her.

I called her into our bedroom and we sat down on the loveseat where she liked to snuggle.

"Devon, baby, come sit on my lap."

Her eyes went wide. She knew something was wrong.

"What, Mamma?"

"Baby, you know how Mimi's been sick?"

"Uh-huh. She has cancers. I know."

The lump in my throat began to ache and tears poked the backs of my eyes.

"Well, it's getting a lot worse, and it's making her really weak and sad. Her body is so sick that it's too tired to help her to get better anymore."

Her brow was concerned. She tilted her head to the side.

"Does it hurt her?"

"Mm hmm." I sniffled. "She's really, really sick."

She tucked her head under my chin and I stroked her blonde hair and tried to speak. I felt my throat closing up and heard my voice turn into a wobbly squeak that I could not control.

"Honey, she'll probably be going to Heaven soon."

"How will she get there, Mamma?"

She paused for a minute as realization dawned and then looked up at me. "Is she – is she gonna DIE?"

I nodded. "Probably so, baby doll."

Her blue eyes were wide and starting to turn pink around the edges with tears.

"But why, Mamma? I want her to stay here with me!"

"I know, baby...me too."

We sat there and I hugged her close and rocked her, wishing I could command the sadness to leave, but it surrounded us like a suffocating cloud.

"Mamma?"

"Yeah?"

"I bet Jesus really needs her there."

"Why's that, baby?"

"Well, she's such a good decorator. I mean, she made her and Pawpaw's house look like a palace. I bet Jesus needs her to come up and help him decorate the mansions because she's so good."

She started to get into the idea. "Probably he needs her to do a whole mansion in zebra print."

"And decorate a whole couch with diamonds," I said.

27

"Yep. And Jesus probably needs a fancy toilet with a crown painted on it. Get it, Mom? It'll really be a throne then."

She giggled for a second and then drifted off in sad thought.

"I already miss her," she said. "I wish she didn't have to go."

Her voice trailed away and then I heard a small whisper, "But I don't want her to hurt anymore."

"I know, baby. Me neither."

"Can I send her notes now and then? Maybe tie them to a balloon and send them to her that way? I don't want her to get too lonely for me."

Right then I wanted to weep loudly and kick the walls and tell God what terrible timing He had. Instead, I held a little girl close as tears trickled down my nose.

"I think that's a wonderful idea, Devon. In the meantime, why don't you go ahead and write her a really lovely letter while she's still here? That would make her very happy."

"Okay. I'm gonna get started on it."

She handled it better than most adults. She understood it. It hurt, but she would adjust. Right then she wanted to tell her Mimi just how much she was loved.

A few short weeks later, Mimi was gone. Her house was silent and sad and heavy. There were no more giggles. The soft music she once loved to pipe through the house was mute. Our family was wrapped in deep grief.

The night after she died, I walked outside her house with Devon. She was not there during Mimi's final moments and did not get the chance to tell Mimi goodbye before she died. We headed down the hill toward the horse barn. The evening sky was clear and the air was chilly. I shivered in the wind as Devon climbed up on the gate and held onto the steel bars. Her six-year-old frame hunched over the top and she stared first at the stars and then at the horses who came close to examine us.

"Mamma, is Mimi already up there in Heaven? Is she really gone from here?" she looked back at me and her voice trembled.

"Yes, baby."

I stood next to her and laid my hand on her shoulder.

"Mamma, I just wanted to see her one more time before she went to heaven." She scowled and jabbed her index finger in the sky to emphasize her words. "Just one more time."

She clung to the gate and rested her blonde head on her arms. She began to wail in earnest and her boots kicked the gate. I stared up at the cedar trees on the hill as her tiny voice howled in despair for many minutes. I was helpless.

She turned and launched herself off the gate toward me. Her glasses were foggy from tears. I caught her mid-air and held her close.

"I'm sad, Mamma." Her voice was muffled in my shoulder.

"I know, baby. I know." I rocked her and rubbed her back as she wept. Her arms clamped around my neck. Her silky ponytail blew around my face and tickled my nose. I shut my eyes and my own tears fell and dampened the hood of her coat that enveloped my face.

Her sobs slowed to an occasional shuddering hiccup and then her breathing became even and calm. She let out a sigh and relaxed against me. I looked down at her tearstained cheeks and realized that she had drifted to sleep on my shoulder.

I took a deep breath and carried my sleeping, sorrowing girl back up the hill toward the house as the night wind blew around us.

THE HARD PARTS

My eyes opened as Shane came hobbling through the bedroom door at 3:47 a.m.

"I'm home, babe," he said, "I'm going to ice my legs and then soak in the tub."

Two hours later I awakened as he crawled into bed and sighed in pain.

"Did you take any medicine?" I asked.

"I did when I got home, but it hasn't helped at all." He rolled over on his side and I heard the groans that he tried to hide.

It was his fourth month working the graveyard shift as a custodian for a local restaurant. Giving had reduced drastically at the church, and there simply was not enough income to pay him, so he had to find outside work to help support our family. It was minimum wage, but it was the only secular job he could find where the manager, after knowing his disability, would hire him. It was twenty miles from home. We could not afford childcare, and he worked at night so that the children could be home with me.

He met me at my office at 5:45 every evening to drop off the children. We would talk for five minutes, and then we would part. He would head to work and I would go home. For eight hours each night, he mopped, scrubbed, bent up and down on ankles that were fused, and joints that ached like fire by the time he was finished.

The restaurant sparkled and he was nominated Employee of the Month, but he could barely walk. His work shoes rubbed against the area just above his heels and turned into blisters, then the blisters popped and the shoes chafed against his raw skin. His feet were in shreds. Then he would return home to begin the nightly cycle of alternately soaking his legs in hot water and then icing them for hours before getting into bed. Sometimes he suffered from back pain and would sleep on the couch instead.

When I would get up for work, he would be in an exhausted sleep so deep that I hated to awaken him to tell him goodbye. So we spoke on the phone later during the day. Our interaction consisted of a succession of emails, texts, short telephone calls, and saying hello to each other on the way to work.

On Saturdays, he worked until midnight and then came home to prop up his legs and finish preparing his sermon for Sunday morning. Although he tried to be silent, I could hear him sighing in the other room, trying to sniffle back tears of anguish.

It was physically devastating for him. He lost weight. The dark circles around his eyes from lack of sleep grew darker. His legs were in constant agony. Our marriage relationship was suffering. We never saw each other. There were no date nights. Any time spent together had to be at 4:00 a.m., and that only happened rarely.

And then his hours were cut. The paychecks grew even smaller, and the cost of gas getting back and forth to work outweighed the time he actually spent there. We decided that there would have to be more budget cuts in other areas, and he put in his notice.

He has worked the most unorthodox jobs and had small businesses, always doing his best to support our family. He has sold shoes and bedding out of a trailer on street corners. He has run an online auction store, and he has preached away from our church whenever he has the opportunity. The man can preach. He has an incredible testimony, but he is a living epistle as well.

When his mother, Sharon, was pregnant with Shane, she was prescribed Bendectin, a drug which was given at that time for nausea and morning sickness. Bendectin was on the shelves from 1956 to 1983. After thousands of lawsuits were filed linking it to multiple birth defects, the drug was voluntarily withdrawn by the manufacturer. A historical lawsuit was filed against the manufacturer, but the Court entered a summary judgment in favor of the drug manufacturer due to a technicality involving expert witness testimony.

In short, the plaintiffs lost. There still is no admission of liability from the drug manufacturer. Although a few settlements were reached, there were thousands of other plaintiffs who came away with no award for damages or compensation of any kind. Nothing but glaring deformities. Many of them, including Shane, are still alive today and doing their best to live a normal life.

Prior to Shane's birth, his parents had no idea that there were any problems. They were only informed that the baby was a boy, but no indications were given of abnormalities. His mother went into labor six weeks early and delivered him just a few minutes later. His father was several hours away when she went into labor, and he jumped into his car and drove 110 miles an hour, frantic to be at the hospital. When he arrived, the physicians would not allow him into the delivery room.

Shane was born with severe physical birth defects. He weighed only two pounds. His head was misshapen from hydrocephalus, and a shunt was inserted shortly after birth to drain the excess fluid off his brain. His legs were curled forward like ram's horns, and his toes were twisted and pointed upwards toward his knees. There was only one long bone in each of his legs from the knee down. His ankles were fused and did not bend. His arms were short. Each one was a different length and did not bend at the elbows. He had a total of three fingers on his left hand, and only one finger on his right.

His parents were blindsided. They underwent genetic testing to rule out any hereditary anomalies, and the tests came back negative. The physician met with them and informed them that Shane probably would not live. In his human wisdom, the doctor stated that if Shane did survive, he would be a vegetable for the rest of his life. The doctor's official diagnosis was that Shane would never walk, talk, see or hear. There appeared to be no hope for him. But the physician did not take prayer or faith in God into account.

Sharon was brokenhearted and still in

shock when Mike went into her room to comfort her. They sobbed and prayed together and their grief over the sad physical condition of their baby weighed heavy upon them.

Then she looked up at her husband and said, "You know, I have a lot of questions, but the only thing I can think of right now is a song about being willing to do whatever it takes to be closer to God."

And so she sang it.

After that first incident, Sharon stopped crying and focused her energy on fighting for Shane.

Around the world people began to pray and trust God for a miracle. In the hospital, a thoughtless nurse broke the hearts of Shane's parents by spreading a rumor that Shane's parents did not want him and were going to give him up.

Shane survived the trauma of birth, and he remained in the hospital for six weeks. There was no brain damage. While he was still in the hospital as a tiny newborn, the first of many osteotomy surgeries was performed on his legs. His legs were manually broken bit by bit and then reset and placed back in casts in order to begin to shape his legs into a semblance of normalcy. The surgeries were excruciating.

In just a few short years, his health insurance was maxed out.

With the help of bulky metal leg braces, he was able to walk by the time he was four years old. A bilateral medial release surgery was performed on the sinews and bones and nerves of his ankles and feet in an attempt to straighten out his feet, and then his ankles were fused to allow him to have some stability.

As he grew older and heavier, the single bone in each leg bowed under his weight and caused him extreme physical agony as the joints and bones in his ankles scraped together in a limited range of motion. His legs and feet were covered with scars from countless surgical procedures and he walked in a careful hobble.

His mother was a feisty little spitfire of a lady. With her tough love, she taught him not to feel sorry for himself, but rather, to learn alternate ways to take care of himself. With only four fingers, it was a challenge for him to tie his shoes. So she showed him how to cross his legs so that one foot rested on his opposite knee. He would lean forward and hold one shoestring taut in his mouth while he wrapped the other string around and looped it into a successful bow.

He still ties his shoes that way today. When Devon was still a toddler, she would watch her father closely as he put on his shoes, then she would grab her own tennis shoe, lean over and put one string in her mouth, and then twirl the other string around and around with both of her hands as fast as she could, grinning up at Shane as she tried to be just like her daddy.

Because his arms did not bend, it was difficult to bring food all the way to his mouth. He learned how to feed himself by holding a fork in his left hand and then pushing his left arm toward his mouth with a shove of his right hand.

While other boys were wearing out the knees of their jeans, he wore out the seat of his pants scooting down stairs on his backside because of the pain in his feet.

Shane was five years old and he liked McDonald's, so his family went to eat lunch there one day. As they entered, they walked by a table full of men, who immediately began to stare at Shane and whisper. His father noticed, but decided to let it slide as he sat down inside the booth. A few minutes later Shane got up to walk to the restroom, and the men began to point and laugh again.

His father bolted up from inside of the booth. Instead of climbing over the other members of the family, he took a shortcut and climbed on top of the table. He let out a mighty roar of anger as he began to run across tabletops in the restaurant to get to the group of people mocking his son.

The men saw him coming and decided it was time to make a quick exit. They scuttled out of the restaurant and ran. He chased them until it became evident that he could not catch them, and then he returned, panting, to the restaurant.

Shane never grew very tall. At thirteen years of age, after countless surgeries to break and re-break his legs, he was still less than five feet in height.

His father met a kind businessman one day on the golf course in Gladewater, Texas, and shared Shane's story. The man's heart was touched and he made it his personal mission to help get Shane admitted into the Scottish Rite Children's Hospital in Dallas, Texas. From that point on, Shane received the finest medical care in the world, free of charge.

It was at the Scottish Rite Hospital that he went through his last surgery. The Ilizarov procedure involved breaking the bone in his right leg again, inserting screws through the leg above and below the break, and placing the leg in a large metal frame. The doctors taught Shane how to turn the screws every day to stretch the broken bone apart. This created a space for new bone to grow and allowed his leg to lengthen, which was comparable to his leg being newly broken every day.

Every time Shane turned the screws, tears would run uncontrollably down his face. The procedure allowed him to grow two additional inches, and he finally attained his full height of 4 feet, 11 inches. He was in the hospital, with few visitors, for a long, lonely period of seven months.

Those times of painful isolation during this crucial developmental period of his life produced a quiet, stable, introverted young man who exhibited grace during extreme difficulty. He observed and listened and had compassion for the hurting.

Six weeks after leaving the hospital, his casts were removed. He was stir-crazy and longed to go play basketball with his friends. His mother finally grew exasperated and told him, "Fine. But if you break your leg, you better not come running back to me for sympathy."

Within an hour, his father received a phone call.

"Dad, I need you to come get me," Shane said.

"What happened, son?" he said.

"I broke my leg again," was Shane's reply.

His leg was shattered and he had to be hospitalized again. But he survived, and he healed and he went back to playing basketball, which is still his favorite sport today.

At summer camps, he was the star of the show, playing basketball and baseball like a madman, putting other kids to shame. He was fiercely competitive. He could throw a football forty yards on a rope with his three fingers. He learned how to water ski by hooking his right hand through the loop of a towel and performed amazing acrobatics on the lake. He conquered the fine art of shaving by pushing a disposable razor down over the end of a toothbrush, which doubled the length of the razor, and then he was able to reach his face and neck.

He never complained about the intense physical pain that he suffered daily from walking and running on feet that did not bend. He hid the emotional anguish that he felt from the stares and comments that were an everyday occurrence, and rarely broke down in front of anyone.

At the age of 16, he felt God's calling upon his life to be a minister. Once he stepped on that path, he never looked back.

He attended Indiana Bible College and

was elected class president. After leaving college, he began preaching and sharing his story with those around him, and opportunities to minister around the world began to present themselves. Shortly after we were married, he flew to the Philippines, Japan and Singapore to speak at various crusades. He went to South Africa for another crusade a few short years later.

Shane has never allowed anything stop him. In spite of unbelievable challenges, he has blazed through barriers of preconceived opinions. When life tells him, "You can't," his response is, "I will." And he does, every single time, with grace and humor and patience.

When our drummer stopped attending church, Shane took several lessons and began to play the drums. He devised a method of wrapping a bungee cord tight around his right arm, which only has one finger and cannot grasp anything. He slips the drumstick underneath the cord so that it is secure and held fast. And then he sits at the drums, playing during church service, worshiping, as tears run down his face.

At this point in his life, he has evangelized around the world, spoken at countless schools and community events about learning to overcome life's challenges, and now is a successful pastor at the church that we planted several years ago. He is a brilliant preacher who speaks with an unusual depth of wisdom and anointing. He loves to skydive and scuba dive, and he is wildly in love with our three children.

He is humble and quiet and he stoops forward in pain, but the fire of determination burns in his blue eyes. He is a giant to me.

I'm just the lucky girl who snagged him.

THE GREAT TOILET CAPER

Gage had always been fascinated by soft rolls of toilet paper and loved unrolling them into large cloudy piles around the bathroom. Just after his fourth birthday, he began to show more interest in its actual use.

I was buried in work in the upstairs office and oblivious to everything outside of the computer screen, when I heard the yell.

"Mom! Mom! The bathroom is flooding!"

Devon shrieked and danced. I came down the stairs to behold a small river winding a lazy course into the dining room, and immediately ran for the shop vac.

Gage stood in the corner of the dining room, hands in his pockets, trying to twist his face into a nonchalant expression. He was trying much too hard to play it cool. In the midst of vacuuming up the water, it hit me.

"Gage Michael Chance! You get over here right now!"

I put on my most stern expression and pointed to a spot in front of me. He shuffled to the bathroom door.

"Did you do this?"

"Did I do what?"

I pointed an angry finger to the football-sized wad of wet tissue that filled the toilet bowl.

"That."

"Mom, I really don't think so. I believe Boy did it."

He pulled his hand out of his pocket and cupped it up next to his face as he peered into his empty palm at his imaginary friend.

"Boy? Can you hear me? You can? Did you make that mess in the bathroom?"

He held his hand up to his ear, wrinkled his eyebrows and listened intently, then shook his head with a regretful expression.

"I'm having a hard time hearing him, Mom, but it sounded like he said not to spank me."

I swallowed the belly laugh that was starting to spill out and bit my cheek in an attempt to maintain my composure.

"Gaaaage?" My voice went up at the end of his drawn-out name.

His shoulders heaved in a huge sigh and he looked down at his feet.

"Okay, Mom. It was me." He held up his hands apologetically and shrugged. "Boy told me he wanted to go to China, so I flushed him down the toilet, and I sent a roll of paper with him in case they don't have paper in China."

He wrinkled his nose and looked up at me with an uneasy grin as he waited for the axe to fall. His glasses were smudged and tilted at an angle over his freckled nose, but they did not hide the expectation of punishment in his face.

I could no longer hold in the howl of laughter that came bursting out of me.

"Okay, dude," I said, "Let's talk about how much toilet paper you need to use. If you keep doing this and using an entire roll of paper every time you use the bathroom, you'll flood the entire house."

He looked grave and thought for a moment.

"And then the whole house would smell like poop, wouldn't it, Mom?"

"Most likely, yes." My giggles were returning.

"I promise I won't do it anymore." His words came out in a mumble from the side of his mouth.

"Okay. Good idea," I said. "In fact, the most paper you need is a piece as long as the length from your shoulder to your fingertips."

We practiced measuring pieces until he got the hang of it. I was secretly proud of the "shoulder to fingertip" method that I had devised on the spur of the moment, as well as the fact that I had put the fear of God in him.

We had no more overflowing toilets for several months, and I was satisfied that he had learned his lesson. Until I discovered his next strategy.

A few weeks later, some Very Important Guests stayed at our house for several days. When they left, I began to straighten up the house, including the upstairs restroom.

I happened to open the cabinet door under the sink and my nose was immediately assaulted by a harsh, grotesque fragrance.

I sat back on my heels and stared with my mouth hanging open. Nestled underneath the sink in the guest bathroom was a pile of used, dirty toilet paper wads, at least a foot high.

I had been wondering why, for the past few weeks, I kept finding dirty toilet paper in the most unorthodox places, the bathroom vanity drawer, in the toy box, and stuffed behind the toilet at church. It had really puzzled me, until now. I had an epiphany. I had found Gage's stash.

"GAGE!" I yelled, "Get up here! Now!"

He bounded into the bathroom and then came to a screeching halt as he saw the open cabinet door.

"What is this?" I glared at him.

Silence. He pressed his lips together and refused to respond. He glanced at the pile of paper and quickly averted his eyes as his ears turned red.

"You have two seconds to answer me."

He opened his mouth to speak and then hesitated again. "It's my paper," he finally whispered.

"Why haven't you been flushing it, honey?"

His sincere expression began to quiver and his mouth turned down into the exaggerated frown of a circus clown.

"Because I didn't want to flood the whole house and make it smell like poop." He began to sniffle back tears.

"But baby, you could have thrown it away in the trash. Why didn't you do that?"

He began to wail in earnest then.

"Because the trash can is bro-ooo-ken!" He sobbed and leaned his head into the corner of the wall.

And that is when I realized he was right. It was my own fault. I had forgotten to replace the trash can in the bathroom after it broke one day. At four years old, at least he was doing his best to try to dispose of the tissue where it would not be seen. I put my arms around him and squeezed him close.

"I'm so sorry, buddy. I'm getting too old and my brain forgot to remind me to get a new one. You want to go to the store with me to pick out a new one?"

He nodded against my cheek and brightened up immediately. "Uh huh! Yes! Can we get one with a superhero on it?"

Disaster and heartbreak were averted, and the mystery of the toilet paper wads was finally solved. And I was so grateful.

* * * * *

Then one day, the toilets died. One minute they were all running just fine. The next minute, water came shooting out of the back of the tank in Devon's bathroom. The downstairs one stopped up so quickly that the dining room was completely flooded in two minutes. The one in the master bath began rocking precariously on its foundation without warning anytime it enthroned a backside, and the tube on the back of the tank started to leak out onto our beautiful wood floor.

The lids on all three toilet tanks mysteriously cracked in half a few days later, leaving the inner workings exposed in all of their rusty glory. Although we pulled up the carpet in the downstairs bathroom, a dank, sour smell began to seep through the house. The broken toilets were evil. The carpet was ruined. The upstairs bathroom tile was swelling up. We were being invaded. It was a hillbilly's nightmare.

This posed a serious problem for the entire family, especially in the middle of the night when an urgent need arose. The boys were okay. They could find a bush in the backyard, but that did not work so well for the girls.

We learned how to turn the water on in Devon's bathroom for individual use, and then quickly turn it back off to prevent it from spraying the entire bathroom and dripping through the ceiling onto the dining room table one floor below.

We could not have guests. There was no decent bathroom available.

The house was fourteen years old. Perhaps because the toilets were in their teen years they just decided to be cantankerous all at once. Whatever the case, none of them worked any longer.

We had no extra money. Shane is a preacher, not a plumber. He tried to fix them, but those attempted repairs ended up causing even more flooding. When he took the downstairs toilet off of its foundation, we did at least discover that it was stopped up due to a 5-inch long seashell that Benjamin had flushed down several weeks before.

I couldn't stand it any longer. We were up a creek without a pot. I began to scour the classifieds, trying to find cheap toilets. New toilets are not cheap.

After constant searching for several weeks, I finally found an ad on craigslist.

"Toilets. Excellent Condition. $30."

My heart stopped. I clicked the mouse. There it was, the ad from Heaven:

"I have 3 toilets for sale @$30 each or make me an offer for all 3. They are in excellent condition as you can see below in the picture."

My eyes glazed over as I stared at the photo. There they sat in all their porcelain glory. Three gorgeous white thrones, containing ample room for posteriors of every imaginable size, and in excellent condition.

I closed my eyes and heard the perfect vibrato of angel voices pouring out in rich, splendid harmony inside of my head. "WAAAAAHHHHH."

I grabbed my phone and immediately called the listed number, praying that no one else was as desperate for three toilets as I was. Now to see if I could get a little bit of a bargain.

"This is Robbie?" The man answered in a very thick accent.

"Yes sir, I just saw your ad on craigslist." I tried to act as if I bought toilets in bulk all the time. "I was wondering if you might still have the toilets available?"

I tried and failed to suppress the squeak of desperation that came out at the end of my question.

"Oh. Oh, yes. I do."

"Well, I was wondering if you might be willing to take $75.00 for all of them."

"Only seventy-five dollars? Hm. I do not know." There was silence on the other end of the line for an eternity, and my heart beat faster. "Well. I guess you may have them for that. They just sit in my garage anyway. You pay cash?"

The angel choir started up in my head again.

"Oh, sure. Absolutely. That's great. Can I come by tonight to pick them up?"

"Sure. I am home after five."

I walked around in a happy daze all

afternoon. I called my parents and told them about the great deal I got. I posted it on Facebook. We were going to have working toilets again. Toilets that simply sat and flushed and did the job they were meant to do. I was teary with relief.

The workday was over and I went to get Shane's truck from his job. I loaded up all three kids and raced away. We were supposed to meet the man at 7:45 that night.

A high-pitched grind sounded when I touched the brakes, and the truck jolted with pain. I moaned. "Not now, God. Please."

God obviously decided to let me figure it out.

A quarter of a mile down the road the grinding started up again and I knew that I could not drive the truck with the children in it. It was too dangerous, regardless of our need for new toilets.

I sighed inside and turned the truck around to move everyone back over to my little Volkswagen Jetta. I was going to be late picking up the new pots, and had no idea how we were going to fit them all in the car, but I was determined to get them.

I called the man. "Robbie? The brakes

on my husband's truck went out, so I will be a few minutes late."

"Okay. See you in the few minutes."

I switched the kids to my car once more and we shot out of the parking lot. My heart pounded as I wove in and out of traffic and out into the hill country. The subdivision entrances became larger and more grand. The houses were spaced further apart. I came to the entrance of the subdivision and scooted through behind a resident who did not appreciate my tailgating.

The kids gasped at the houses we passed. Like mansions they were. Golden lights shone from the porches onto the perfectly manicured lawns. I had a happy feeling in my heart. These were going to be some lovely thrones.

We pulled into the driveway and the good man was standing with his hands in his pockets, waiting for us. The sun was almost completely gone, and the sky was beginning to turn purple.

He politely ignored the loud clanking of my engine as it idled and smoked in the driveway and shook my hand. He squinted at my car.

"Where are you going to fit everything?" he said.

"I'm going to squeeze in everything I can, and if I can't get it all in tonight, I will come back tomorrow and get the rest, if that's okay with you."

He led me into the garage. There it was. The toilet in the picture. *Hello, my beautiful,* I thought. I wanted to kneel down and put my arms around it.

He demonstrated that the lid opened and closed properly, up and down, up and down, and explained that all of the necessary parts were included. I nodded, back in my happy place.

"The other two toilets are across the street. How about if you take those tonight, since they are already in parts, and will probably fit better in your car that way."

"Sure. Let's do it." I floated back to my car and chugged across the street to his neighbor's house.

A beautiful elderly lady stepped out of her front door and glanced sideways at the automobile in her driveway that was causing so much racket. She shook my hand while Robbie stepped into the garage and came back with his hands full of toilet parts.

"Here. We can put those in the trunk." I opened the trunk and heard a small gasp behind me as the old lady saw the heaps of toys and clothes piled inside.

"I'm sorry about the mess." I felt my face turn hot. "I don't think I will ever catch up and be organized until I am dead and six feet under."

"Dear, just be patient," she said. "It's those kids you've got. Stop worrying about it."

We fit one toilet bowl into the trunk and Robbie went back into the garage to retrieve the other one. He came back out to the car with the other toilet bowl and looked at me with a question in his eyes.

I opened the back passenger door and said, "Let's stick it right here next to my son."

His eyebrows shot up. Madame Old Lady began to wring her bony hands. "My dear, do you think it's safe?"

I was pretty sure it wasn't. I was also determined that I was not leaving without at least two complete toilets that night.

"Here. I'll put it in a seatbelt. Like this."

I bent over to fasten it in and felt eyes boring into my hind end as my two spectators looked on. I clicked the belt and smacked the toilet with a nonchalant "we're all set here" sort of whack.

"Alright. Let's go."

"Mom?" Gage looked up at me with his mouth open and patted the toilet bowl sitting upright next to him.

"Yep."

"Do I get to ride with this next to me all the way home?"

"Yes you do, honey. Isn't it great?"

"Oh yes. Yes it is, Mom." He gave me a pleased nod and sat back with a grin.

I stood up and shook the hands of my toilet angels. My heart was full of gratefulness. I turned to climb into the car. They stood there together, the tall young doctor and the short, frail old lady, with expressions that told me something was still undone. I waited.

The good man finally placed his hand on the back of his head and blew out a sigh as if he even hated to bring it up.

"Did you want to go ahead pay us now, Miss, or wait until tomorrow?"

My cheeks turned hot. "Oh! Yes! I am so sorry."

I dove into my car and grabbed the money, which bounced out of my hand. Three $20's, one $10 and five $1 bills went flying all around the dashboard. I didn't dare turn on the interior light because they would have seen the interior ceiling in my car which had fallen down some months back and was beginning to take on age spots. I poked around in the dark and finally assembled all of the money.

I handed it to the doctor and turned to get into the car. He had his head down counting the money and did not look up as I drove away. The old lady turned around and grinned at us as we clanked and bounced down the road away from their subdivision.

"Mom! I want my ice cream now, please!" Gage had been so patient.

"Okay. Let's go to Chik-Fil-A."

"I want McDonald's." His lip started to tremble, and I remembered that I only had some change and would have to dig around for more.

"Alright. We'll go to McDonald's."

We pulled into the drive-through and I

waited for the attendant. Silence greeted me. I waited for another five seconds.

"Yellow?"

The children started to giggle.

"Yell-o. Breaker Nine One Five. Yell-o. Anybody home."

"Sorry for the wait." The disembodied voice squawked out at me. "What can I get you."

I looked back at the kids and whispered, "Watch."

"Uh, yayess sir. I will take ONE of them VERNILLER cones."

The kids snorted and began to laugh quietly. Silence from the other end of the microphone.

"What was that, ma'am?"

"I'll have ONE of your ver-NILL-er cones, if you don't mind."

"Just one?"

"That's right, son."

"That'll be $1.08. Please pull around."

Explosions of laughter rocked the car as we pulled around. "Mom! Ask him for moist towelettes! Ask him for red ketchup!"

"Indeed I will not," I said.

I soberly handed the precious counted pennies to the young man in the drive-through window and he waved me on to the next window.

I glanced sideways at my offspring, who waited to see what would happen next.

The second window opened and out popped a vanilla ice cream cone.

I looked at the cone and shook my head sadly. "Oh, mayam. I'm afraid I'm gonna have to ask you something."

The second attendant tried to show me a concerned expression. "I'm sorry. What?"

In my most solemn voice I said, "I'm gonna need about five of them nakkins you got there on that cabinet."

I heard muffled snickers of glee in the car behind me. "Mom said 'nakkins', Gage."

More giggles.

I caught the napkins as they sailed through the window.

"Thanky kindly, young lady."

I pointed my noise in the air like a haughty queen and we drove away in grand style as the kids collapsed in laughter.

LET ME HOLD YOU

Gage is a two-year-old container of undiluted joy. Blonde and built like a diminutive linebacker, he races madly through his miniature world, oblivious to peer pressure, the stock market's volatility, or the prospect of world war. Sorrow has little effect on him. His crocodile tears last for an instant, and then they are gone. Like a tiny caped avenger, he streaks past in his diaper and cowboy boots, constantly moving, searching for exciting moments and shiny bugs.

He delights in throwing spaghetti in his sister's hair, pulling the heads off of her dolls, and stealing her lip gloss for his own personal use. He cocks his head to the side like a puppy and watches in fascinated stillness as an ant climbs over his foot. His happiness is complete when he wriggles his toes into his racecar slippers and has me wrap his Spiderman blanket around his body.

He is like a small tornado, whirling his way through the day, leaving a path of destruction wherever he goes. I happened to glance up the other day as he flew by me, pretending to be a dinosaur. The afternoon sun outlined a crouching, growling silhouette, and his hands flailed the air above his head in little claws as he hopped full speed ahead toward the light, roaring with all of his strength.

He loves ferociously. My husband took a break after wrestling with him the other day, and said, "Gage, you rock!" Gage stopped stock still for a moment and then shrieked at the top of his lungs with happiness. He whirled around, vehemently pointed both index fingers at Shane and yelled, "You rock too, Daddy!!!"

It is impossible to clean house unless he is asleep, yet, when I see him lying there like a rosy-cheeked angel, it is equally impossible to continue cleaning. My arms ache to hold him. His baby soft skin has yet to become weathered by the elements, and, when I hold him close, he feels like warm velvet. I am head over heels crazy about my little man.

Maybe it's the way he looks at me and creases his face into his "squishy grin," a smile so wide and huge that the muscles in his cheeks force his eyes to squeeze shut. Or it could be when he crawls into my lap, buries his face in my neck in a fierce hug and whispers, "Now, dis here, dis is my woman."

I think what really dissolves me into a puddle, though, is when he walks up to me, turns his face skyward, extends his arms, hands, and fingertips as straight and high as they can go, and in his low, tiny voice begs, "Mamma, lemme hold you. I wanna hold you." His blue eyes implore, and he leans in close as his entire body pleads for me to pick him up.

The world can be in crisis negotiations, our church in uproar, and every outside influence hammering at my soul, but when I hear those words, "Mamma, lemme hold you," time stands still. Every position I hold loses importance, the pot bubbles over on the stove, and the unfinished project gets pushed away. My "mamma" radar hones in on the one who needs me. Nothing else matters.

I bend down toward him, and his eyebrows lose their concerned lines. I gently lift him up into my arms, and my heart melts. He burrows his face into the hollow of my neck between my collarbone and shoulders and relaxes against me with a shuddering, happy sigh. There is no pain, nothing to be tense over, or worried about. He is in my arms, and that is all he wants. Oh yeah. Life is good.

As I held Gage the other day, I was struck with the amazing simplicity of his need for me.

There are no strings attached; he just wants me for me. He needs to be near me, even if just for a few minutes. Those times strengthen his assurance that I love him and fulfill his need for closeness.

Oh, if only I would take the time to approach my Heavenly Father with the same abandon and lack of pretense! As I scurry through my day, He watches me tenderly through gentle eyes of love, smiling at my peculiarities and sometimes moved to tears by my infirmities. He loves me with a love beyond compare.

Every void, every place of need, every area of my life that lacks affirmation and acceptance, He longs to satisfy. I am His child, His beloved. Yet I neglect my precious time with Him and continue to run on, attempting to cover my empty soul with a mask of wit and sophistication. While I spend my life getting and pursuing and chasing, my Greatest Fulfillment silently waits for me, yearning to hold me, aching to wrap His arms around His child.

So often I forget to seek after those valuable, stolen moments, when I am His and He is mine. Then my strength fails. I crash, completely exhausted, wounded, and destitute. And that is the point where I remember again my deepest need of all - spending time with my Father.

Murrell Ewing so eloquently described it when he sang:

Sometimes the little boy in me
Wants to climb on my Father's knee
When the world outside
Gets too big for me
When the fear's too much
For me to hide
And my finest dreams have almost died
He always understands me when I say

Hold me, hold me
I'm so afraid of the storm
Hold me, hold me
I'll be safe in my Father's arms

Oh God, let me approach you like a child who is unable to bear the weight of the world. Please hear my broken whisper as I hesitantly stumble toward you with arms outstretched as far as they can reach, "Let me hold you, Jesus. My heart hurts. Please make it better."

Let me close my eyes and lean against your chest, wrapped in the warmth of your arms, knowing that I can trust you with my tears. Let me hear your soft, whispered reply, "I love you, daughter. You are beautiful and you are mine."

Father, please help me remember that I can't live without my time with you. I need to hold you.

STALLED OUT

Devon was finally interested in the toilet.
She was almost two and it was time. We were
traveling around the country as evangelists, and
staying in different places with new people every
few days had taken its toll on potty training. This
stuff was difficult.

I tried to bribe her with M&Ms and
Cheerios, but did not realize that I should wait
until she finished. There she would stand in the
restroom, hold out her hand for me to give her
the candy, and then happily walk back out,
clutching her prize.

Lugging a potty chair in our truck
everywhere we went was nasty. We finally found
a little seat that was foldable and fit right on top
of the toilet. She loved it. The wheels of potty
training were finally in motion.

She sat there dangling her feet and bopping her head up and down. She clapped her hands and squealed.

"Oh! I'm a big girl now, Mahmah! Look. I go potty! Where's my candy?"

Success. Finally. I felt immense relief and wanted to jump and scream with excitement.

"Mamma is so proud of you, baby! You ARE a big girl! Yay!"

Each time we visited the bathroom after that, I clapped my hands with her and we celebrated with appropriate exclamations. We were making progress.

Several weeks later, we were at a restaurant and made our way to the crowded restroom. I took my turn first.

Inside the stall, Devon's tiny head only reached the bottom of the toilet paper dispenser. She stood motionless in front of me with a rapt expression, and then began to jump up and down, clapping her hands.

"Ooooh, Mahmah! You SUCH a big girl.... I so proud of you! Oh MY.... Wow! WOW! You doin' GOOD!"

The decibel level of her voice could have

pierced concrete walls. I heard snickers from outside of the stall and felt my face turn purple. I closed my eyes. In my mind I tried to go to a secluded quiet forest where no one knew me. It did not help.

I heard my low reply come from somewhere far away, "Thank you, baby."

She waited for a moment, then reached out and patted my arm. She leaned forward and stared up into my eyes with a look of deep concern.

"Mahmah? You need help with the paper? Here. LEAN UP, MAHMAH. I HELP YOU." She pulled at my hands. I felt a burst of tingling embarrassment in my feet and uncontrollable laughter began to bubble up. I tried to keep my voice level.

"You're very kind, baby. I think I'll be fine."

"Mmnph!" I heard the stifled snort from somewhere outside the stall and then an outright giggle.

She was puzzled.

"Why they laughing, Mahmah?"

"Because they think you're cute. I do too."

"Oh. Okay." She shrugged her shoulders and pursed her lips in a "fair enough" gesture. She considered me for a moment and then gave me a sweet smile.

"You have a big bottom, Mahmah."

My mind went numb and little spots swam in front of my eyes.
"Yep."

I knew the situation would only grow worse if I didn't think of something quickly.

"How about we get some ice cream when we get out of here?"

"Yay!"

She pumped her hands in the air and stood on her tiptoes with a look of supreme happiness. Her concerns about my restroom needs were forgotten.

I slowly blew out a sigh, straightened my shoulders and rolled my head around on my neck before opening the stall door. We marched out of the stall with our heads held high.

One little white haired lady was bent over the sink, wheezing with laughter. "Ohhh! Hooo hooo hooo!"

Several other women grinned broadly at me as we washed our hands. I grinned back through the red splotches of mortification that dotted my face and neck and tried to recover.

We dried our hands and Devon looked up at me with a smile. She pulled my hand against her face and shut her eyes for a second. Her wispy pigtails brushed against the back of my wrist. I melted.

I put aside my humiliation to revel in the moment. I scooped her up and put her on my shoulders. She shrieked happily and pounded the top of my head with her fists as I carried her out, tall and proud.

THE PREACHER'S SEAT

Spicewood, Texas is a dusty spot in the road. There is no stoplight. Time moves slowly and the people do too. The heat does that to you.

The original Baptist church that my great grandfather attended as a child is still open. The town hosts an annual Homecoming every year where the old men stay up all night to smoke brisket that will make you cry with happiness, and women proudly display their famous casseroles and Jell-O salads that hide unidentifiable fruit and nuts.

Families are deeply rooted. Jeans and cowboy hats are the common dress code whether you are 18 or 85 years old. The only store, Hollingsworth's Corner, changed its name about twelve years ago to Spicewood General Store, but no one has ever called it by the new name.

When you say you grew up in Spicewood, people invariably say, "Oh, you mean Spicewood Springs?" To which you reply, "No. Spicewood. It's off Highway 71, about 15 miles from Marble Falls." This response is usually met with a moment of puzzled silence then a sudden grinning nod that attempts to mask the fact that they have no idea where Spicewood is.

If you take Spur 191 down towards the old post office and turn right at the Y towards Krause Springs, about a mile out is a little dip in the road, sandwiched on each side by a 5-foot deep creek.

This is James Burton's Creek. At least that's what we always called it growing up.

It was the creek of all creeks.

If you drove too fast and hit the dip when the water was over the road, you might flip your car, or at least cause it to stall out and die. Giant old trees whose roots snaked through the creek bank soared into the sky about a hundred feet it seemed, and sunlight fought hard to get through the thick curtain of greenery.

In times of drought, a thick slime that looked like pink vomit would cover the surface of the creek. When the water was running, though, deep green shadows and faint spots of light bathed a quiet pool and created an idyllic sanctuary. Even on the hottest day, the water was cold enough to cause goose bumps.

Slimy lichen and moss-covered rocks just under the water were hazardous to unsuspecting feet and tender backsides. A rickety old wood picket fence tied together with wire sagged sideways across the creek about twenty feet away, protecting the property of a long-dead land owner from a bygone generation. Tadpoles darted in and out of the rocks. Dragonflies swooped and the bushes rustled with lizards and shy creatures of the underbrush. Birds called out to each other in alarm. As swimming holes went, it was just about perfect.

Many lazy afternoons were spent there, floating and looking up at the clouds that showed through the trees, and having picnics, eating tuna sandwiches on the bank. Few cars ever passed by. It was just me, my sisters and my mother, who would not let us get in the water until she combed our hair into French braids so tight that our eyes were pulled back at the corners. And then we swam like little fish, with no fear of snakes or slime or unseen horrors of the deep.

On a scorching day in June, we moved from Texas to Michigan to go pastor a church. That afternoon before we drove away, my mother piled us into the big Buick and took us to the creek for one last swim. Nanny, my grandmother, came with us. We snuck onto private property a little further down the creek and parked behind a fence so that no one could see us. The sun burned hot and lit up the water so clearly that we could see to the bottom.

Nanny sat in the front driver's seat of the car with the door open and watched us as we splashed happily and talked about all of the packing that we had accomplished and the toys that we had to leave behind. I tried to show off my swimming skills for Nanny and began to brag about my ability to swim on my back.

I turned to jump back into the water and I heard her quiet voice.

"Have you ever done the Preacher's Seat?"

"Huh?"

"The Preacher's Seat. I used to do it when I was young."

"Um...no." I was embarrassed to admit that this was one dive I had never heard of.

She got out of the car with her mouth set in a firm line and walked over to the edge of the bank, her hands planted on her hips. At 66 years of age, she looked like the epitome of a grandmother, soft and approachable, with wrinkled hands, kind brown eyes, and gray hair beginning to fade to white. She was dressed that day in her standard uniform, a long navy blue skirt, long-sleeved shirt buttoned up to her neck, brown hose and blue SAS shoes. Her hair had just been fixed and sprayed at the beauty shop.

She stood there surveying the water for another moment and then gave a determined nod.

"Well, you do it like this," she said.

We all whirled around and stared.

She kicked off her shoes.

One second my grandmother stood at the edge of the creek bank peering down at the water. The next instant, she soared into the air in a sitting position with her legs straight out in front of her. Her toes were pointed like a ballerina.

Time stood still as she sat solemn and erect, suspended in the air three feet above the water. Her head was tipped upward in a stiff, exalted composure, nose aimed at the sky. Her expression dared anyone to laugh. Her arms were thrust straight out to the side, level with her shoulders.

She hung in the air for a moment and then plummeted straight down into the water, still in a sitting position, and landed with a mighty splash that rivaled every cannonball I had ever attempted. My mouth hung open and I watched through water-logged lashes as she stood up and made her way, dripping, back to dry land and began gravely to wipe the water and dirt from her stockinged feet.

The spell was broken and we all immediately began to try to imitate her. She did not do it again. To this day, I still cannot see how she managed that particular feat. She made it seem so effortless. When I tried the Preacher's Seat, I began to understand how it came to have that name. The water stung my backside and slapped against the backs of my legs like a thousand freezing cold needles. Although I practiced many times in later years, I never could quite get the rigid posture that was needed to land on the water, still sitting straight up.

We left that night for Michigan and left our childhood behind. As an 8-year-old child, I did not realize that it was the end of innocent childhood or that our lives were about to change drastically. I did not notice the sadness that hung heavily between my mother and grandmother, nor did I feel the sharp ache that comes with the realization that we were about to be separated by over a thousand miles.

Some moments are so vivid that they burn into your memory forever. My grandmother's abandonment of all composure to bring amazement and delight to her granddaughters was a brilliant flash of an instant that will never go away. It was her parting gift to us. In my mind's eye, I will always see that portrait of Nanny sitting in the air with her eyes closed, just above the icy cold water, a tranquil smile on her face, arms held out, suspended in time, with the sun dappling her hair and the gold field as a backdrop behind her.

THE DEMON BALL

I rubbed my heavy eyes and leaned back against the chair to stretch. The laptop light burned in my face. The room around me was shrouded in the deep dark that comes from having no windows. An enormous yawn engulfed my jaws and tears pooled in my eyelashes.

At 3:27 a.m., it was deathly quiet in the church evangelistic quarters where we stayed that cold January. Shane and Devon snored in the bedroom as I worked on the internet, transcribing police interviews and court hearings. It was my way to help support our family.

I was grateful for the job that I could take on the road with us as we traveled and preached. It was flexible and I could work at night while the baby slept. Depending on where we were that week or month, my options for an office setup were limited.

Sometimes all I could do was sit on the floor with my laptop and headphones, pressing my foot pedal against the wall as I transcribed vehement denials and violence and learned about the underworld of crime and drugs and gang slang. It was hard, demanding work, but I did a good job. I was proud of myself.

This particular night was no different.

I sat back after finishing up an interview of a murder suspect. Even though I typed like lightning, the job had still taken over six hours to transcribe. My hands and wrists tingled and throbbed, and my entire body ached from lack of sleep. I was done. I submitted my job and went offline.

When we traveled, we always brought a box of toys for Devon. At 16 months of age, those toys were her constant in an ever-changing environment. She loved them.

Her favorite was the alphabet ball, covered with letters that stood out in bas relief. If rolled on the floor, it sang the ABC's. If a letter was pushed, it would obligingly bawl out the letter's phonetic pronunciation, "Aaaaay. Beeee. Ceeee." Devon shrieked with delight as she played with it for hours.

I had not replaced the batteries in the alphabet ball for several months, and it was dying. New batteries were not the top priority on my list. The alphabet ball currently resided at the bottom of the toy box and occasionally would bump into other toys, at which point a low, mournful groan would issue forth from the bowels of the toy box.

That night I decided to tidy up the room before stumbling into the bedroom. The only light left on in the room was a small night light. I shuffled around in the gloom, picking up Devon's dolls, books and teddy bears. I counted the seconds until I could collapse on the bed.

My eyes started to roll back in my head as I began to dump the pile of toys into the toy box. My body was shutting down and I sighed, thinking of the big soft pillow just a few steps away. I smiled in the darkness as the toys landed in the bin.

Some people derive utter peace and vast fulfillment from staying in the church evangelist's quarters. I am not one of those individuals.

I do not enjoy walking through dark corridors at night to find the restroom, nor do I find creaks in the rafters soothing. Dark churches, especially at night, are not places of quiet rest for me. I always have the urge to shriek and gallop away as fast as I can from that deep foreboding Something that seems to sail with tattered wings in the shadows behind me, hovering, waiting to perch on my shoulder with its foul claws.

I stood in the living room by myself that night, wobbling with exhaustion and let the toys drop from my tired arms into the toy box.

Out of nowhere came a loud, sepulchral cry that rose up into the darkness.

"WooooowwAAAHHHAARRGGH."

It wrapped itself around me, and then died away into silence.

All of my senses clanged as my eyes flew open and I swayed backward. My heart clenched painfully somewhere in the back of my throat as I went into fight-or-flight mode. Visions of unseen phantoms swam in front of me. I was suddenly airborne, frantically pedaling backward and flailing my arms, my mouth wide open, trying to get away from that moan of utter horror.

I shrieked at the top of my voice. In my efforts to scramble backward from the sound that embodied every fear that I had ever imagined, my feet became entangled in the hems of my baggy pajamas. Down I went, kicking, thrashing and yelling.

In the bedroom Shane heard my howls of terror and came thundering to my rescue. I sat curled up on the floor next to the toy box as the light came on, and cried tears mixed with dread and relief.

"What's wrong? What happened?"

Trying to understand the commotion, he stood there helplessly, staring at me.

"I don't know." My voice quavered from shock. "It just – I was – it was dark -- and then something groaned at me. I don't kno-o-o-w-w."

I started wailing again and leaned back against the toy box in limp relief.

"Wooooooahhhh."

There it went again.

My heart stopped beating and I looked up at Shane with a wordless plea for help. He gave a half-hearted shrug and kicked the side of the box with his bare foot.

From the recesses of the box, the battery-deprived demon ball began to sing a jagged, warped version of the alphabet song.

"Now I know my A-B-Ceeeee's. Won't you sing along with meee.... me.... me...me..."

I slept that night with my face planted in Shane's chest and vowed to find a new home for the alphabet ball as soon as the sun came up.

PLANTING A NEW BABY

Starting a brand new church. Five little words that carry so much weight, so much burden and hard work, but we did it.

We finally stepped out in faith and began to walk in the direction that God beckoned. We said yes, two young, naive people with two small children.

We had the nice house, two cars, two well-paying jobs, savings and retirement accounts, and impeccable credit, but we said yes. Shane gave his notice, and a short time later we packed up his office at the church where he had been the assistant pastor for the last five years.

We began to plan the launch of the new one. We never looked over our shoulders. We had no one to fall back on, so we began to travel and evangelize to supplement the loss of Shane's income, and to build up a foundation of financial support for the new church.

The personal attacks on us began. Phone calls flew around and rumors traveled and hearts broke and tears fell.

But we still kept saying yes.

On Easter Sunday, we held a preview service and over 50 new people visited. We were excited. Our little group had a good thing going. We strategized and dreamed and life seemed rosy. Our church was about to be launched.

Sickness and exhaustion began to set in and I noticed that I could barely keep my eyes open or my thoughts focused. On Mother's Day weekend, the pregnancy test came back positive.

Just a few weeks later, we were approved to launch our new church. We held our very first service as the Sanctuary of San Antonio. We met in a little room in the Hilton Airport Hotel. The sound system screeched and shorted out and the younger children clamored and distracted the adults, but we cried tears of gratitude that God had brought us to this place. We were official.

The new life growing inside of me sucked the life out of me. I tried to smile and be a good little pastor's wife, but sometimes the smile didn't reach my eyes. The tiredness was overwhelming. All of the planning and working toward this place of fulfillment had forced me to push aside the ache in my heart, but now that the busyness had quieted down, the ache was back. I tried to swallow it and keep moving forward, but it bled through everything.

I was still working full-time. I had never stopped. Our savings were dwindling, and I was grateful to have a job that helped support our growing church. That all changed in June when I lost my job.

Three months pregnant, I was stunned and paralyzed. We were completely unemployed. The new church was small and could not support us full-time. I began scheduling interviews for a new job, and worked at home in the meantime doing online transcription. But with two children tugging at me all the time, and heavy with the third, I barely made enough money to justify the time I spent working. It was a vicious cycle.

I would put on my interview suit that was stretchy in the stomach area, jam my swollen feet into high heels and go out to yet another fruitless interview. No one wanted to hire someone who was expecting a baby. I had never had a problem finding a job before. My confidence was shot and I was exhausted. After over 30 interviews I finally told God, "I'm through. I've prayed that you would lead me to the right place, so please do that. I've used up too much gas and time trying to find a job, and I just can't do it anymore."

I cooked a lot of beans. We sold household furniture to make ends meet. I developed amazing recipes from the strangest ingredients and made up fascinating names for those dishes so that the kids would eat them.

We swallowed our pride and filled out applications for Medicaid and nutritional assistance. At least the children would have fresh fruit and vegetables to eat, and they would have medical insurance.

As happens with any new church startup, some of the people who were helping us to start the church decided to leave. When that happened, the income at our church decreased even more.

But we kept saying yes and having service every Sunday morning. Our new people loved it. We were penniless. Our savings were gone, our own mortgage payment was starting to fall behind and our credit score was spiraling downward.

Every service, I waddled to the keyboard and played and sang my heart out and led worship. Shane preached and people were blessed and changed.

In late October of that year, Rev. Carlton Coon, our national director for North American Missions, came and spoke at the Sanctuary.

We had a total of $17.00 cash to our name. Our bank account had less than $5.00. There was simply not enough money to take him out to a restaurant for dinner when he came to San Antonio that afternoon. I used the cash to buy what groceries I could, and cooked a meal for him at our home. I remember that he was extremely gracious and complimented the food, but my exhaustion almost overwhelmed me. My memory of the rest of that evening was a blur.

The next Sunday morning prior to service was a disaster.

We had no other food left at home. I was running late and the kids were hungry. As we attempted to have music practice before service, Gage began to howl.

"I'm hungry, Mahmah! Now! I need food!"

He rolled around on the floor and squalled. An old lady sitting in the back began to glower at me. In my eighth month of pregnancy, I was severely hormonal and my heart began to thump. I took her expression personally and just knew that she thought I was a terrible mother. I stopped practice, picked up Gage and marched out to the hotel snack bar to buy him something to eat.

My bank card was declined.

My heart sank. I had no other money. I turned away from the puzzled attendant and walked away holding Gage, trying to stay composed.

He howled louder. "Mahmahhhhh! I'm so hungry!"

I took him into the ladies restroom and stood in the stall as I began to sob uncontrollably, horrified that I was not able to feed my son.

It was 9:55 a.m., and church was starting in five minutes. I was shaking and losing control. I knew I had to calm down, because there was no one else to play the keyboard or lead worship service. If I didn't show up, no one else was going to.

As I walked back into service, our youth pastor immediately assessed the situation. He held out his arms for Gage and took him from me to go find a snack. I gave him a grateful smile. My face was splotchy and red and I looked like I had been hyperventilating.

Rev. Coon was walking in the door at that moment, and I managed to give him a very watery greeting.

Service began with a beautiful worship song about God being "faithful, ever true." I closed my eyes and tried to control my emotions, but anger came to the surface as I thought, *God, how on earth am I supposed to believe that you're faithful, when we don't even have money to buy groceries for our children? What are you going to do about us? We've given everything we have to get this church going, and now we have nothing left.*

Sitting at the keyboard, I faced the congregation. There was nowhere to hide. My voice quavered and shook as I played the keyboard and sang. Unwanted tears began to run down my face and plopped onto the keyboard. My cheeks were twitching from the pressure of holding back sobs. I was mortified, but there was nothing I could do.

The next song was, "Jehovah Jireh, my Provider."

I shook my head as I sang. *What on earth was I thinking when I put together the song lineup for this morning?* I wanted to sit down on the floor and wail, but I had to finish leading worship service.

I kept singing and playing the keyboard and weeping as I tried to tamp down my emotions and get to the end of the song. I knew that I looked like a soppy mess. I felt like I had completely embarrassed our church in front of our national missions director. What a first impression.

Curling up and dying sounded very nice, but I tried to take myself away to another place and forget about our circumstances. This was worship service and I had a job to do.

I happened to look up.

Lo and behold, people were worshiping. Some were crying. Our esteemed guest speaker was doing an exceptional job of hiding his dismay over the pastor's wife who was having a nervous breakdown at the keyboard. He was, in fact, raising his hands and worshiping. I looked around. The entire congregation was on their feet worshiping, and there was a sweet presence of God. I was amazed.

After church was over, our guest speaker thanked me for leading worship the way I did and for ushering in the presence of God. I almost fell over backward. My emotions were still fragile and I was afraid to say much of anything because I knew I would break down into tears again.

I learned that morning what it really meant to offer up a sacrifice of praise. That is truly what it was. A sacrifice. I gave everything I had to lead worship, including the anger and fear, and God moved in spite of me.

And we survived.

Three years later, the Sanctuary is beginning to thrive. We are in a new building, a home of our own. Every tear, every bit of heartache has been worth the new souls that have been reached in our city. And that is what it's all about.

THE OTHERS

When we launched our new church, we were very green and inexperienced. We thought that everyone who came through our doors would be simply hungry for God, without any outside agendas. For the most part, that was true.

And then there were the others.

I sat in church that winter morning holding a newborn Benjamin. Ted came hurtling into the ballroom where we were holding services. He rode in his wheelchair, hunched forward like he was in a race, his feet swinging noiselessly above the floor. He wore a newsboy cap over a military buzz. His whiskered cheeks were sunken and leathery.

His hands shoved the wheels forward and he sped up the side aisle on a mission, making a beeline for me. He lurched to a violent stop in the aisle and parked himself next to my chair. I turned toward him to say hello and he shoved a hand toward my shoulder area. I reached over and shook it.

"Ted Perkins, ma'am. Retired special forces, ma'am," he spoke in a growling whisper. He stared into my eyes for a long moment and then inspected the room in sections before turning to listen to the speaker with an intent gaze.

A few moments passed. The Sunday school teacher continued speaking, and all was silent. Ted began to fumble around in his pockets and pat his pant legs. A low chuckle started at the back of his throat.

"Heh, heh, heh."

He began to shake his head back and forth and then reached over, clutching my arm. I felt a chilly discomfort in the pit of my stomach.

"Ma'am."

"Yes?"

"You've taken my cell phone."

I was puzzled. "No, sir. I don't have your cell phone."

His voice grew louder. "Yes, ma'am. You did. You stole my !@#$*&% cell phone."

People were beginning to turn around and stare at us. I was thankful to have men in the room who were willing and able to remove unruly individuals.

"I'm sorry, sir," I looked him in the eyes, "I really don't have your phone."

His lips drew back against his teeth and he hollered out, "YOU STOLE MY !*&#$%^ CELL PHONE!" Flecks of spit landed on me.

A hush fell over the room and everyone turned to watch the show. Ted glowered at me and I could see madness in his eyes. I knew that I needed to remove myself and my baby before he tried anything dangerous, so I muttered something about going to ask the usher if he had seen any phones, and quickly scooted away with Benjamin in my arms.

Ted rolled out behind me and began asking the usher for money from the collection plate for cigarettes. When the usher refused, Ted changed his tactic and said he actually needed money for his prescriptions. When the usher again refused, he wheeled himself out of the sanctuary and began to ask people in the lobby for money, orange juice and cupcakes. He never came back inside, and ultimately wheeled himself out the front door and down the street.

Unbeknownst to me, Ted had already displayed some unique behavior earlier that morning. Shane had gone in his truck to pick up Ted for church. A strange odor pervaded the interior of the truck. When they arrived at church, Shane went around to the passenger side of the vehicle to help Ted. He removed the wheelchair and unfolded it.

Ted stood up and got out of the truck, then turned backward and looked down at his chair before he sat, considering it for a moment. Shane's eyes followed him and came to rest upon the stunning object of his focus.

In the wheelchair sat a large pile of drying, slightly squashed excrement.

With solemn dignity, Ted reached into his satchel and pulled out a bottle of hand sanitizer gel. He reached down, and as if creating an ice cream cone, squirted the gel around and around in meticulous circles on top of the pile and finally emptied out the bottle with a swirling flourish. He pulled off his wool neck scarf and carefully scooped the contents of the entire pile off from the chair into his scarf. He gave the chair one last smearing swipe and straightened up.

Shane stood frozen as Ted suddenly

pulled his arm back like a baseball pitcher, lobbed the feces-saturated scarf into the back seat of Shane's truck, and slammed the door.

Not a word was exchanged between them as Shane helped him into his chair. Ted wheeled himself into the lobby and began his expedition towards me. Shane opened the door and lowered the windows to allow some airflow into the cab, and then carefully extricated the offending scarf from his truck interior.

After church was over, Shane's eyes were round with disbelief and he waved his arms around as he described his adventures with Ted.

"Randa, it was terrible," he said, shaking his head. "I've never seen anything like it. He threw a poop scarf in my truck! In my nice, clean truck!"

"Well," I said, "I apparently stole his cell phone too. I thought he was going to choke me or try to grab Benjamin in the middle of church."

And so go the exploits of the church planter. Some things that happen in real life are simply too wild for the imagination. You meet all kinds, both the wonderful and the crazy, and you live to tell about it. And those memories live on forever.

* * * * *

When Margaret walked into church for the first time in her tent dress, long red cardigan, and crocs with socks, I thought I was seeing Drew Carey's nemesis. She was built like a linebacker. The layers of fat on the backs of her arms were solid slabs.

When the usher tried to shake her hand and welcome her, she bared her teeth and stuck her face two inches from his nose.

"You can just shut up and stay away from me."

He backed away with a polite bow and let her go into service.

She never would provide her contact information to us, but she did come and introduce herself to me that first Sunday. She stood there holding her chin between her index finger and thumb and contemplated me for a moment before closing her eyes momentarily.

"Now," she said, "I wanted to come talk to you first and meet you, because a lot of women have a problem with me talking to their husbands. I'll let you tell your husband that I've come to church today."

I assured her that I would do just that, and

refrained from saying that unless someone's vision was severely limited, there would be no problem noticing that she was in attendance.

Her ultraviolet purple eye shadow covered her entire lids, from brow to lash, and the sparkles could be seen from forty feet away. She wore a pair of large plastic glasses that dangled from a chain around her neck. Her backpacks were full of used items that she wanted to donate to the church. She typically came in mid-way through service and dragged her belongings up the aisle to the front row.

She always waited until church was finished, and then would motion me over so that she could display the contents of her backpack.

"I clean houses, you see," she would whisper, looking over her shoulder to make sure no men were listening, "And things just COME to me."

She nodded and beckoned toward herself with pudgy fingers as if she were sweeping cobwebs into her bosom.

I'll bet they sure do, I thought.

"I donate these things to churches," she said. "It's my ministry."

I dared not ask her how or where she

acquired all of the things she brought and tried to accept them gracefully. The torn pieces of bread, handfuls of broken pencils and dirty bath towels quietly disappeared into the trash bin as soon she left. Useable school supplies were sanitized and donated to Sunday school. Shoes and clothing went to Goodwill. The dollar bills and pocket change that she stashed carefully in baggies were put into the offering plate.

She never showed any interest in worship or prayer, but during service, she moved around, straight-faced, with surprising agility. Her necklaces jangled and flew up as she waved and flapped her arms in windmills. She threw her head back and solemnly fluttered her fingers up and down in the air, as if she were trying to do sign language.

When inspiration struck, she would suddenly point at me and nod as I played the keyboard. She would direct the music with accompanying decrescendos and other wild swoops of her arms. Her six-inch bouffant remained intact and only trembled slightly when gusts of artistic fervor shook her round frame.

When asked if she would like to have a Bible study, she shivered and hugged her arms around herself. "Oh no. Ohhhh no! Uh-uh."

When Margaret came to church that last time, Shane was already at the pulpit getting ready to preach. I saw her come in as I finished playing the keyboard.

Margaret decided that she wished to sit in the greeter's chair which was located next to the door. The greeter was already seated there. She pointed at his chair, indicating that she wanted him to move. Instead, he invited her to sit in one of the many available seats in front of her.

She stepped over in front of him and tried to plant herself in his lap. He gently moved her.

She glared at him and then stomped halfway up the aisle and began scattering chairs right and left, five rows from the front, until she found the chair that evidently suited her taste. She dragged her preferred chair all the way to the back, about two feet from the usher, and threw herself into the seat with a huff. She spent the rest of the time talking to herself and cutting her eyes at the greeter.

She waited until Shane finished his sermon and everyone stood. I watched her from my place at the keyboard as she took her backpack, threw it over her shoulder and sashayed out the door with her nose in the air and a distinct wiggle in her wide hips.

Margaret never came back, but I will never forget that period of time that she graced us with her presence. Her jiggling arms and spirit fingers brought some much needed laughter at a time when we were feeling the pressure of pastoring and planting a new church.

She was exactly what the doctor ordered. She came dramatically into our lives, jolted our attention away from our difficulties, and then made her grand exit without so much as a sayonara.

Sometimes, without warning, angels come on the scene wearing tent dresses with cardigans. And we are all the better for it.

BOBBY PINS, BEES AND OTHER CREATURES

Stress does strange things to a body. Emotions grow stronger, reactions are over the top, and sometimes things are just not what they seem. When I am very tired or under pressure, small things grow into mountains and I feel overwhelmed. In that state of mind between consciousness and deep sleep, the imagined becomes extremely real to me.

Shane and I were traveling as evangelists in the Midwest United States in the dead of winter and my exhaustion had just about reached its limit.

My feet constantly felt like blocks of ice. We were gone from home for months at a time, and the bundles of mail that would come for us did not always carry good news. It was hard being away from home and trying to survive financially.

Although it was fun meeting new people everywhere we went, and we made some friends for life, we did not own a travel trailer. Instead, we usually stayed at the pastor's home or in a room at the church. There was minimal privacy.

If we had a marital disagreement, it was usually carried out in bitten-off whispers in our room and we dared not raise our voices. If the baby cried during the night and would not be quiet, there was always the fear that we were keeping someone else awake in the house. That part was difficult.

One evening, Devon fell at the pastor's home where we were staying and cut open her mouth on a large plastic jug that was sitting on the floor. She was a tiny little pixie of a girl and it was hard for me to see her in so much pain. People hovered around her wringing their hands and hoping she would be okay. I felt like we were under a microscope and I felt my poise begin to crack.

Her mishap was just the tip of the iceberg for me. Multiple telephone calls that day from bearers of bad news already weighed me down, and then Devon got hurt. I picked her up and headed to the bedroom, where I sniffled back the tears that refused to stay put and cleaned away the blood from her mouth.

After getting Devon calmed down, Shane and I finally fell asleep just after midnight. The bed was dreamy. Devon was between us and snuggled close to me. The house was warm and quiet and my toes were starting to thaw. I sighed and sank down in squishy pillows that felt like heaven and drifted away into a Neverland of soft snores and whistles.

I woke up at 3:30 a.m. with a honking snort and sat straight up in bed with a sharp feeling of dread. I began to pant and stared wildly around the dark room.

I became aware of a growing conviction that I had just swallowed a metal bobby pin in my sleep, and it was too late to do anything about it. My throat had already closed around it and I felt the pin as it traveled down my esophagus.

I clawed at my throat and began to cough in panic. Nothing happened.

I climbed forward on the bed and got on my hands and knees. With my head hanging down, I started to hack like a cat with a hairball, trying to gag up the bobby pin. Five minutes of retching produced no results. I tried kicking my leg high up in the air behind me at intervals to try to dislodge it, but stopped after I knocked a picture off the wall with my foot.

Jumbled thoughts began to run through my head.

Oh, Lord. It's in my sternum by now. This bobby pin is going to go down into my stomach and pierce my intestines, and I am going to die from a severe infection. God, don't let me die this way.

I started to cry as I gagged, still on all fours.

My baby is going to grow up without a mom. My poor Devon. I'll miss you so much.

Devon started to stir next to me and I was reminded that others were in bed. I realized that I still had another option. Shane was there. He could pray for me.

He lay there, sleeping so beautifully. His mouth hung open wide as he sprawled out, sawing gigantic logs in blissful slumber.

I leaned over and whacked him in the stomach with one hand as hard as I could, still trying to maintain my balance on my hands and knees.

An unconscious bellow came squeezing up out of the depths of his abdomen. "HUNNHH!" His head lifted slightly off the pillow from the force of my punch.

He laid there, his eyes rolled back in his head. He was not waking up.

"Shane!"

I prayed that my frantic whisper would not be heard down the hall. No response.

"Shane!"

"Whahh? Huh?"

His bleary eyes rolled around to look at me and he struggled with a grunt to sit up in bed. He turned on the lamp next to the bed and glanced at his wild-haired, mad-eyed wife who crouched on the bed, alternately weeping and gagging.

"Oh, Shane!" I cried, "You have to pray for me right now!"

Shane is a quiet sort of guy who rarely loses his cool. He sat for a moment observing my frenzied cough-gag-wheeze routine and then calmly asked, "What's wrong?"

"I've swallowed a bobby pin," I sobbed, "And I'm going to die if I don't cough it up."

I have to give him credit for not roaring with laughter in my face. He reached over and gave me a pat on the shoulder.

"Babe. You're dreaming. Lay down."

"No, I'm not! I swallowed it in my sleep and then I woke up too late to stop it."

I turned and looked at him over my shoulder and pleaded, "Please, please pray for me. I don't want to die."

The mixture of terror and tears and mucus drainage on my crumpled face must have convinced him that I was in earnest. He blew out a longsuffering sigh and walked around to my side of the bed.

Laying his hand on my back, he began to pray. "God, please touch Randa right now."

"HOOAAAARRACK!" I started trying again to heave up the foreign object.

"Take away the pain and fear and give her rest."

"OOOOAAAAAAAGGGGGHHH!" I stopped caring about whether anyone else in the house could hear, and howled out a pitiful groan.

"God, please let her go back to sleep and if there really is anything wrong, please heal her."

He wrapped up his prayer and rubbed my

back for a moment. I collapsed on the bed on my stomach and laid there with my face in the covers.

Even in his sleepy state, Shane still managed to produce a few tears of sincerity as he prayed, and that comforted me. Maybe I was going to be okay.

"Go to sleep, hon," he said, "You're going to be fine. I've prayed for you."

"Okay. Thanks," I said, my mouth muffled in the comforter, "I really appreciate it. I really do. I love you." My eyes teared up as I voiced my gratitude.

He rolled his eyes at me as he shuffled back around the bed, turned out the light and slid under the covers. His breathing soon turned into peaceful snores again. I lay in bed wide-eyed and stared at the dark ceiling, trying to stay awake just in case Death arrived and I needed a second to try to tell Shane and Devon goodbye forever.

Finally, my eyes grew heavy and my addled brain decided it might be easier for everyone if I were sleeping when I slipped away into eternity, so I closed my eyes and left my fate in the hands of God. I rested well.

The next morning the sun hit my eyes and

I awakened. I remembered my terror in the middle of the night and felt mortification as I began to laugh. I sat up and looked over at Shane, who was watching me out of the corner of his eye.

"So," he grinned at me. "How are you feeling?"

"You can just be quiet now, sir." I said.

For the rest of the day and several weeks after, whenever I came close to Shane, he would start to chortle and then his exaggerated hoarse falsetto would follow after me.

"Oo-oh! Pray for me, dear. I've just swallowed a bobby pin!"

* * * * *

In a chilly November, Shane and I returned home with Devon from evangelizing. We found a tiny one-bedroom apartment to live in while we saved money to buy a house. Our little family crammed all of our earthly belongings into 650 square feet and did our best for a year to make it work.

The apartment was so small that the laundry closet was just outside on our three-foot-wide back porch. Devon slept in our bed, and we stored our belongings wherever we could find an empty space, under beds, under the sofa, and behind the couch.

Laundry was my nemesis. I hated stepping out onto that freezing cold concrete to wash clothes while people across the lawn from our apartment watched from the comfort of their living rooms. I would scuttle through my chore as quickly as possible and then pirouette back inside.

I opened the laundry closet door one day and noticed some small insects on the ground next to the dryer. Closer inspection revealed dozens of bees, nonchalantly walking around on the floor and crawling up under the wall. That concerned me. I was allergic.

Just on the other side of that wall was the headboard of our bed. I could imagine bees crawling out through the electrical plug sockets and stinging us to death in our sleep. I called the apartment manager and requested that someone come deal with the bees.

Two weeks passed. Despite my repeated calls, no one came to fix the problem. The bees were multiplying, and it became obvious that they were building a hive inside the wall.

At night in bed, I could hear tiny chewing sounds directly behind my head and I would lie awake, staring wide-eyed up at the ceiling. I worried that one day they would chew through the wall and a cloud of bees would invade the bedroom, and there we would be. My anxious musings always ended there, without any sort of contingent plan.

Finally the midnight buzzing and chewing grew too loud. I was done with providing free rent to bugs and tired of waiting on maintenance. I went to the store and bought some bug bombs. I had never used them before, so I purchased four. Surely all of that smoke would be strong enough to make some bees cough and die. I never thought about the fire hazard or the danger to the human occupants of the house. God was merciful.

That night before going to sleep, I went to the bedroom and stood listening to the happy hum coming through the wall as the bees chewed and worked on their hive. I taped up the electrical outlets in the house and then went outside. Time for war.

I opened the laundry closet door and watched as scores of velvety bees crawled back and forth under the bottom of the wall, blissfully unaware of their approaching doom. I set off the bug bombs next to the opening in the wall. Smoke started to billow out and I shut the doors as quickly as possible, stuffing towels underneath. I ran back inside to wait for the bees to croak.

Several minutes passed. I still could hear chewing and crawling. I sighed to myself. *Oh well, I tried. Tomorrow I'll just call an outside exterminator.* I turned around to walk into the living room.

The gentle droning in the wall suddenly increased in decibel to an angry buzz. It grew louder and higher with each second. The pitch became more shrill and I knew that the bees were starting to feel the effects of the smoke as they swarmed inside the wall. I yelled for the others to come to the bedroom.

"Shane! Devon! Get in here! Listen to this."

We sat on the bed and stared at the wall behind the headboard. The furious whine of hundreds of bees held steady for many minutes as we prepared for bed. I was so glad I had thought to tape up the outlets.

The wall continued to whine and vibrate half an hour later as we climbed into bed and tried to sleep. The noise level was slowly beginning to lessen, but the bees were fighting to stay alive.

I lay awake and listened, so proud that I had conquered the bees. Finally I would be able to sleep without the fear of insects invading our home. *You are a mighty bug killer,* I thought to myself, and realized that I sounded like a cheesy motivational recording.

The roaring buzz eventually died down to a sick whisper, and then faded away altogether. The wall behind us had finally become a tomb for insects, and I was filled with the immense, drooping relief that comes after a long bout with stress is over. I drifted into a deep sleep.

About 1:00 a.m. something awakened me. I opened my eyes and looked around without moving. The streetlight filtered through the window and created a pale luminosity in the room. I could see the wall to the right of our bed.

My sleepiness faded away and my heart began to hammer. The gray wall was freckled from top to bottom with hundreds of tiny black dots, and the dots were slowly moving around.

I was frozen momentarily and watched the dots from the corner of my eye without moving my head. *Dear Jesus. The bees. They are inside. We have to get out. We have to go now.*

"Shane! We have to go! Get up!"

My whisper was urgent and I could feel all of the blood in my body pounding in my hands and feet.

I frantically reached for Devon, still trying not to make any sudden moves. I whispered desperate prayers that the bees would not be startled and start attacking.

In my heightened state of panic and tired confusion, the only thing I could grab hold of was the apple of Devon's cheek. I pulled upward with all of my might. She sat up with a pained expression and looked at me with a whimper as she covered her cheek with her hand.

"Ow, Mahmah. You hurt me."

"I'm so sorry, baby," I whispered, "We have to go."

My entire body was shaking as I scooped her up and ran out of the bedroom. She was only wearing her diaper. I had no idea where we were going to go. I just had to remove her from danger.

I reached the front door. The only shoes there were my six-inch heels, but they would have to do. In the darkened living room, I began to shove my sock-covered feet into the shoes as I held Devon on one hip and reached for the car keys. I turned around as the light came on in the bedroom.

Shane was leaning against the door, just

watching me. I looked at him, shocked, and started to cry. I knew the light was going to wake up the bees and they would be flying out the bedroom door toward us at any second.

"Shane! What have you done? Why did you turn on the light? We have to get out!"

I stood by the open front door, shaking in my pajamas and high heels, ready to run out. I begged him to leave with us as tears streamed down my face.

He scratched his head and stayed where he was.

"Randa. Come get back in bed."

"No! The bedroom is full of bees! We're all going to be stung. I'm—"

"Randa." He was magnificently serene as he looked at me. "There are no bees."

"I'm allergic. I'll puff up like a marshmallow." I continued to sob and babble as Shane walked across the room toward me. "They must have climbed through the electrical outlets. I don't know how else they could have gotten in!"

"Randa. You're having another one of those dreams again. There are no bees. They all died."

"But I saw them. I SAW them! They are all over the wall!"

Shane was so patient. He took my hand and said, "Okay. That's fine. Just come look and see for yourself."

I laid Devon down on the living room sofa so that she would be safe. I wobbled back to the bedroom door in my socks and heels. Hanging onto Shane, I slid my nose around the edge of the door and took a stealthy sideways peek.

Huh.

The light was on and the wall was empty once again. No bees. Not a one. I looked around the room and shameful realization began to dawn.

"See? I told you. You're dreaming again." Shane gave me a tired smile and walked past me to fall across the bed. "I'm going back to sleep. You're welcome to join me."

"I'm sorry." I stood there, feeling incredibly stupid and embarrassed about my sleepy hallucinations. "Let me go get Devon and we'll come back to bed."

The light went off. We climbed back under the covers and my heart rate slowly returned to normal.

The next morning I went and inspected the laundry room. The little room smelled like pesticides. Piles of dead bees covered the floor, and I was happy again. Crisis averted.

The bees never returned. (And I suppose if I were a bee and saw four bug bombs neatly lined up next to my potential new place of abode, I probably would stay away too.) The night terrors have returned occasionally, and I have "swallowed" other things in my sleep like dice, car keys, and even a twig, but none have since been so vivid as the bobby pin or the bees.

TRIALS BY FIRE

"Um, Daddy? I think something's burning."

Gage shuffled into the living room and stood facing Shane with an expression of studied nonchalance.

"What do you mean, son?"

Gage shrugged and replied with his mouth twisted to the side, "Well, it just smells like smoke in the kitchen,"

Shane ran into the kitchen. Sure enough, next to the island was a three-foot fire in the plastic trash can, burning higher by the second. He grabbed the sink sprayer and managed to douse the fire before it incinerated the island. He turned to Gage.

"What did you do?"

Gage looked him in the eye and tried earnestly to lie. "I don't know. It was just burning."

"A trash can doesn't just spontaneously combust. Were you playing with matches?"

"Maybe," he whispered and traced a line across the floor with his bare toe.

"Don't ever do that again!" Shane put his hand on Gage's shoulder. "Do you want to burn the house down? We could have been burned up!"

"I'm sorry, Daddy," Gage said. "I won't do it again. The match got too short and I had to throw it in the trash because it was starting to burn my fingers."

Shane sighed and shook his head and prayed for patience as he waited for me to get home from work.

When I arrived, I smelled the burning plastic, saw the charred trash can covered with black smoke streaks. I immediately felt my stomach churn as long-forgotten memories of another fire played in my head. I picked up Gage and carried him to the couch to sit on my lap.

"Buddy, did I ever tell you about the time I burned down my house to the ground?"

His eyebrows shot up behind his glasses and his forehead wrinkled in disbelief. I had his attention. "No way! No, you didn't."

"Sure did. All the way to the ground."

His mouth dropped open and he shook his head. "Wow, Mom. I didn't think you had it in you."

I turned my head away to hide my grin. I wanted Gage to understand how serious his actions were.

He settled back into my arm and listened as I dredged up a decades-old memory that I wished had never happened....

I was four years old. My sister, Krystal, was just three. My family lived in a little old house just off Highway 290 in Johnson City, Texas. The house sat on a concrete slab foundation, a stone's throw across the yard from the church we attended.

The night was clear and cold. We were happily playing in the living room. The Imperials were singing "I'd Rather Believe in You" on the eight-track stereo. We had already taken our baths and were wearing long cotton nightgowns with ribbon bows tied at the neck.

Through the large window opening between the kitchen and living room we could see our mother standing in the kitchen cooking dinner. Her back was to us as she stirred a pot of broccoli. The house was warm and moist and the boiling water and other pots on the stove added to the elevated temperature.

Behind her was the white Formica dinner table with the aluminum band around the edge. To the right was the old refrigerator. It was dark outside, supper was almost ready, and our father was on his way home from his construction job.

While we waited to eat, I grew bored and decided it was time to make up another game.

"Hey!" I said, "Let's pretend that we're Daniel in the lion's den."

"Okay," said Krystal.

She followed me to the large Hide-a-Bed sleeper sofa. The velvet upholstery was covered with brown and orange rural scenes depicting landscapes that included horses pulling carriages. The couch sat against the wall and faced a large window across the room that looked out into the front yard. The window was covered with heavy floor-length pea green drapes.

Crouched in front of the drapes was an old four-legged ceramic heater. It was open in the front and a row of blue and purple flames hissed at onlookers. The heater was turned on.

I grunted as I pulled the cushions off of the couch and threw them to the side.

"Oof. Here, Krystal, help me pull out the bed part."

Together, two little girls tugged on the heavy metal folding frame inside of the sofa until it finally slid up and out and the hidden bed unfolded onto the floor.

"I'm gonna be Daniel," I said.

I was the oldest and felt entitled to the star role in our playacting. Krystal went right along with it.

"I'll climb under this empty part up here where the bed used to be, and that will be the lion's den," I said to her.

"You can be the king and come look for me. So, when I climb under here, you need to come and yell, 'Daniel! Daniel! Are you alive?' and then cry and get happy when you see me. Okay?"

She nodded and grinned, excited about

the new game. The only hitch was that the polyurethane mattress on the bed inhibited my progress down to the hollow part of the couch where the sleeper sofa usually resided.

I slid my arms underneath the mattress and used all of my strength to scoot it off its metal frame and then pushed it up against the wall, where it stood completely covering the old heater. Satisfied, I climbed down into my hidey-hole and became Daniel, waiting to be eaten by lions. I crouched and waited for the king to call on me.

I realized after a moment that there was no yell from Krystal. In fact, there was no sound from her at all. I stuck my head out of the cavity to see what was holding up our game.

Krystal was mute, scampering back and forth on the top of the couch behind me like a tiny squirrel, her eyes wide with terror.

I froze as I saw the mattress propped against the wall across from me, covered in flames that were silently licking their way up the drapes. Paralyzed, I watched as the fire climbed the curtains and began to spread across the ceiling above us.

In a matter of seconds, the fire gained strength and began to crackle and then roar in the old living room. The heat became oppressive, but I could not move or speak as the flames completed their track across the ceiling and then began to race down the wall next to us.

I will never know whether it was the increasing crackle of the flames or the hot glare reflecting on the wall that made my mother turn from the stove to look at us.

She screamed, "Jesus!" and dropped her spoon. She ran into the living room, pulled me out of my cave, and grabbed Krystal. We started to shriek as the rest of the living room began to spontaneously erupt into an inferno.

"Go, go, go!" she commanded, "Get out! We have to go now!"

She dragged both of us out the front door as the fire roared higher behind us, and we ran barefoot, stumbling, into the front yard. I felt weak and wanted to lie down.

"Girls, we have to go next door to Becky's house to call the firemen. Come on!"

My mother and Krystal frantically ran in front of me and I tried to keep up with them. The ultraviolet light from the street lamp illuminated Krystal's thin nightgown and pale blonde hair with a greenish glow as she held my mother's hand and ran forward in the night on her tiptoes.

My mother hammered on our neighbor's chain link iron fence and screamed, "Becky! Open the gate! Hurry!"

Her voice broke as she began to sob. "Please unlock the gate!"

Becky came running into the yard to open the gate and stared agape as the howling flames began to shoot through the roof of our house. My mother sobbed hysterically on her shoulder and Krystal and I huddled close to her skirts and looked back at the house.

The timbers of the old structure whined and then began to fall inward. A thick smoke that smelled of burning wood, melting plastic and roasting electrical wires filled the air. In just a few short minutes, flashover occurred and the house exploded in heat. The fire department arrived quickly, but too late to save anything. We watched from the safety of our neighbor's yard as firemen scurried around like ants to keep the fire from spreading.

My father saw the orange glow in the night sky as he drove home from work. His concern turned into overwhelming dread as he grew closer and saw the sparks flying and realized it was our house that was burning.

Frenzied thoughts screamed through his head as he spun into the driveway. *My family.*

My babies. I have to get my family out. I have to get them out. He jumped out of his Toyota pickup and his frantic body met with the immovable Pat Jennings, a nurse who attended our church. She blocked his way with her girth and outstretched arms. He fought to squeeze past her and she wrapped her arms around him in a crushing embrace to stop him. He struggled against her and Pat shouted at him to get his attention.

"Don't go in there!" she yelled, "They're out. Everyone is okay. No one is hurt. Everyone's fine."

Pat's words pierced my father's violent hysteria. He realized that we were all safe and came to find us.

Our entire world burned to a crisp that night. All of our toys, clothing, important documents and pictures lay in a charred pile of smoking rubble. All we had left were the clothes we were wearing when we ran out of the house.

The next morning Krystal and I were awakened by people handing us dolls that had been donated by a kind volunteer. Mine had wild hair that stuck out all over its head. It was bald on the back and was supposed to make a crying sound when its stomach was pressed, but what came out resembled a dying, asthmatic wheeze more than anything else.

Krystal's doll had copper wires woven through its hair which turned into curls when twirled into a circle. In the middle of chaos and loss, we were delighted with our new treasures.

When the fire cooled, my parents sifted through the ashes to see if they could salvage anything. They found their wedding album, burned around the edges and streaked with smoke, but the pictures were still intact. That was all that was left.

There was no insurance on the house. We had nothing left to start over, so our little family made our way to sleep on the couch at our pastor's home, and then later, to my great grandfather's house. We huddled close. With no money and with broken hearts, my parents began trying to reassemble the pieces of our world blown apart. It was not an easy time.

Christmas morning came that year.

Relatives came in from out of state to stay for the holidays. Krystal and I had gone to bed wide-eyed and hopeful the night before, with quiet whispers of what might be under the tree for us in the morning. We were only little children, not yet acquainted with the silent overshadowing anguish that lies heavily upon parents faced with sudden poverty, unable to provide for their family.

I opened my eyes that morning to happy sounds and the sight of my excited cousins tearing through wrapping paper that flew around the living room. Gift after gift was opened and tossed aside as they moved on to the next one. I watched them from the couch where I had slept and waited quietly for mine. Nothing ever came. I looked around and realized my parents were not in the room.

I got up and walked into the enclosed front porch that my parents had turned into a bedroom. My mother was silent as she stood at the window with her arms crossed in front of her, looking out at the hills and valleys that could be seen for miles. I did not want to upset her, but I had to know. I tugged on her skirt and she looked down.

"Mamma?"

"Uh huh?"

The loud, happy hum in the living room faded away as I craned my neck back and gazed up at her.

"Did you know it was Christmas?"

I waited, hoping with all of my being that she had not forgotten. She became very still for a moment and then turned and walked away from me to the dresser. She reached down into a drawer and pulled out something that fit into the palm of her hand.

"Go get Krystal," she said.

I ran out of the room and woke up Krystal. We came back into the bedroom and shut the door. My mother held out her closed hands and said, "Girls, this is all I have. But this is for you."

We reached forward and she placed into each of our outstretched hands something unwrapped and small.

I looked down and saw a tiny scented Strawberry Shortcake doll. Krystal received a companion Orange Blossom doll which smelled like a Creamsicle. They fit into our pockets and smelled lovely.

We were extremely pleased and hugged our mother. We took our dolls and sat on my parents' bed in our nightgowns, exclaiming about how nice the dolls smelled. We played for a few minutes as Mamma watched.

I looked up. "Mamma?"

"Yes?"

"Is this all you got us for Christmas?"

She looked down at the floor. I was not intending to make her feel bad. I just wanted to know. I do not remember if I ever even said thank you.

"Yes," came her tired sigh, "It's all I can do right now."

"Okay." I was satisfied and I went back to undressing my miniature doll.

And that was Christmas. We had each other. We were healthy and alive, and we were together, and that was more than enough. It was everything..

LOVE

"Yell-o," I answered the phone.

It was my friend, Becky, a neighboring pastor's wife.

"Randa, I have a question for you. This is our last women's meeting this year at church. Do you think you could come and speak to our ladies?"

A two-second silence ensued as I pretended to check my nonexistent calendar.

"Okay. I'm open. What's your theme?"

"Well, we've been talking about the fruits of the spirit. Can you come up with something along those lines?"

"Okay. I'll get back to you," I said.

I decided to speak on how it is more important to love than any other spiritual gift. It was a subject that I was passionate about.

I was ready to talk about an age-old revelation that had only recently been made clear to me. I felt so enlightened. My own world had changed, and now, hopefully, I was going to help change the worlds of some of the ladies at this upcoming meeting.

The day came. Shane waited until that afternoon to inform me that he was scheduled to work that night. I had no choice but to take our children with me. My hair was sticking up from the humidity. I came straight from my job to meet Shane at our church, collected the children, and then drove to the church across town with three very tired babies who looked like they had just stepped out of a wind tunnel.

Benjamin was barefoot. His shoes had disappeared somewhere deep inside of the chaos of Shane's truck. All three children were covered with Cheeto-tinted powder and red soda stains. Gage was crying. Devon was hot and sweaty. And they were all starving.

Several women from our church decided to come that night, so they followed me across town through traffic that crawled at a turtle's pace and never seemed to end. The whines and signs from my backseat turned into tears and howls.

"Mammaaaaa! I'm hungry! I don't want to go to church tonight. Why do we have to go?"

I tried to calm my nerves and pray quietly as I drove so that I would be ready when we got to the church, all the while passing out snacks behind me to any hand that could reach them, and trying to stay on the road without rear-ending any vehicles.

After fighting traffic for 45 minutes, we finally arrived.

"Okay, guys," I finally said, "Here's the deal. I have to go in there and talk at a ladies meeting. There are not any other kids there and you might be bored. Would you like to go in the nursery and watch a movie on my laptop?"

"Yeah! Yeah! Yeah!" Devon grinned.

"Yessssss!" Gage sat back against the seat and quietly pumped his fist next to his waist as if he had just won a contest, his eyebrows raised in a happy arc over his forehead.

Benjamin looked around at the commotion and gave an affirmative nod, accompanied by his usual "Uh-uh," which actually meant "yes."

It was settled. The wee ones were satisfied. We were going to get through this just fine.

We got out of the car. I brushed off the kids, zipped up Benjamin's pajamas, and we headed inside. I thought longingly of the deodorant and toothbrush that I had forgotten at my office. I would just have to do without and try to remember not to be vigorous with my arm-waving or speak too forcefully, lest I singe someone's face with my breath.

Gage poked my leg as we walked in and I looked down at my curly-headed imp.

"What?"

"I love you, Mahmah."

His freckled face gazed up at me with a lopsided, dimpled grin. My tension flew away into another place and was forgotten as I ruffled his fuzzy curls.

"I love you too, buddy. Let's boogie."

Inside the church we found a hiding place for the kids to perch during the meeting and set up their video. We were good to go.

I stood in front of the mirror and checked for any clothing that might be tucked up where it should not be. I confirmed that my girdle was doing its job. All good. I took a deep breath and put on my smile as I marched in to meet everyone.

We sat at round tables, in a room apart from the main sanctuary, and I realized that the song I was planning to sing at the end of my talk would have to be a cappella. There was no keyboard in the room. *Okay*, I thought, *Just shorten up the song and relax. You can do this.*

I was so glad to have women from our church with me. They calmed me. I sat at the table and prayed silent prayers while Becky introduced me, and then it was time.

I stood up and walked to the front. I was wearing heels. The podium was about hip-level.

"Do you think we can raise this at all?" I asked Becky.

The room was silent as we juggled the telescopic stand, and finally pounded it into submission. I laid down my notes and began.

"Tonight I want to share something with you that has changed my life."

I looked up and saw faces of women in varying stages of life and realized, we are all the same. I forgot where I was and began to speak. Everything faded away, and it was just us in a room so silent that every sniffle and hiccup could be heard.

I came to a point that I really wished to emphasize.

"It does not MATTER—"

I slapped the top of the podium with the flat of my hand.

"—if I possess every spiritual gift that is available. If I don't have love, I am NOTHING."

I was completely absorbed in conveying the message. I stopped and leaned forward and rested my hands on the stand in front of me. I looked around the silent room and made eye contact.

"If I—"

The podium suddenly collapsed down into itself in front of me and came to rest at the height of my knees.

There was a second of shocked silence as I stared down a great distance to my notes, which were still intact. They rested on the podium next to my kneecaps. The room erupted in laughter. The intense moment was gone. I turned red and began to laugh too.

Okay, God. What now? I thought.

Just go with it, I heard His still, small voice. *It's not about you.*

True, I thought. *Off we go.*

I came to the end of the simple message and asked everyone to join hands and close their eyes. Around the room I heard people praying.

I looked up. "We all have our own secret sorrows. Not one of us is exempt from pain. Let's find strength in each other tonight, before we leave here."

Voice wobbled out in tearful prayer and ladies huddled close to each other. I closed my eyes and began to sing from the depths of my soul without any music.

I happened to open my eyes as I sang the next line.

Help me give—

I did a double take and my heart stopped. In the back of the room stood Benjamin, completely naked. The top of his diaper was held up only by his kneecaps.

His blonde hair stood out in a cloud around his head, full of static electricity. A fleeting question raced through my mind, wondering where he had stowed his pajamas. He looked at me with shining blue eyes and his lips moved as he held out his arms.

"Mama," he mouthed. In his eyes was a look that said, "I'm coming to you so you can pick me up and hold me." And he stepped into the room.

Everyone's eyes were still closed. No one saw my naked child yet. I shook my head at him with vehemence and continued to sing, but I sped up the song as I watched him move toward me in agonizing slow motion. Every word I sang seemed like an eternity.

Please God, I prayed, *Let him stay in the back. Everyone is going to start laughing again and that will be awful.*

I sang on and the words began to race faster and faster. Heads remained bowed as Benjamin looked at me with a determined face and began to sidle up behind the curtain that lined the wall, legs held wide to keep his diaper from falling to his feet. I sighed with relief. He was hidden temporarily.

A tiny body parted the curtains at the front of the room, just to the left of me, as I sang the final line of the song. The song was over. Silence reigned again.

Benjamin stepped out and stood next to me in all of his rosy splendor.

"Oh look," a woman said, "Here is someone's baby."

I scooped up my bare-bottomed boy and scuttled toward the back of the room.

"Becky!" I motioned to my friend with panic in my eyes.

"Oh, Randa, can you just sing that one more time?" Becky whispered as she walked by me toward the front of the room.

"Um," I said. "I'm going to sing from the back of the room, so as not to distract anyone, if that's okay."

I stood by the door and held Benjamin in my arms and gave myself a mental kick in the backside. *Time to forget about what people think. My child is in my arms. He is where he wants to be. I will survive. I am his mamma. There is nothing I can do about his state of undress right now.* I began to sing again.

Benjamin hid his face in my shoulder and began to relax as I sang. He had his mamma and he was happy. And, I realized, so was I. I tried not to giggle as I sang, thinking about how all of this must have looked to everyone else.

I finished the song as I rubbed his back and ran my fingers through his blonde curls, and then ran out the back door to dress my son before anyone could remark on the nakedness of the preacher's kid in the church house that day.

NANNY'S HANDS

My grandmother's hands are knotted and gnarled and bent. They are covered with age spots. They rarely sit folded in her lap. They speak her silent language of love instead, stirring a pot of fudge or making a sandwich, cutting and arranging the tomatoes and lettuce just so for the children she loves, or steering madly through traffic and scattering frantic pedestrians.

I look at my own hands and I see how unsightly they are. My hands are small and knobby with thick, wrinkled knuckles and little fingers. They strain to reach an octave on the piano. They are rarely manicured and are the cause of many exasperated sighs. I am the wife of one and the mother of three, and my hands do much work.

They pick up children, and they write. They hold frying pans, and they fold laundry.

They smooth down lumps of hair that got twisted the wrong way. They flail wildly when I talk. They change diapers. They change light bulbs. They change careers. They hold hands, and they smack behinds.

They cup chins and point vehemently. They tickle tired backs. They smooth down and close lifeless eyes at hospital bedsides. They reach further than I would ever think possible. And they are short and stubby.

I have always admired people who have graceful, sensitive fingers. I used to have a strange notion that I could be more expressive and artistic if my fingers were long and had a little downward slant at the ends. I would do my best to gesture with stretched out fingers, hoping that it would make my hands look a little longer.

But glancing down, I see the reality of diminutive fingers and uneven freckles. I see a small callous melded around the back of the finger where my wedding ring has rested for fourteen years. On my left middle finger is a knot that has been there since I was six years old, created by holding pencils and pens too tightly. The unvarnished nails are short and brittle from years of typing and playing the piano. Multiple hangnails abound. No one would ever ask me to be a hand model. My hands are small and quite unremarkable.

Then I look at my mother's and my grandmother's hands and realize that theirs have been passed down to me.

My imperfect hands have held babies and comforted tears and held hearts as they mended and came back together into one piece. My hands have patted bottoms and wiped away tears and checked foreheads for fever. My hands have cradled sorrowful faces and wrapped around shoulders that were drooped in dejection.

I look at Nanny who has held close and laughed and wept over eleven of her own babies and over eighty grandchildren and great grandchildren in her life. I watch her as she holds my youngest son. He nuzzles into the crook of her arm. His bottom lip is sucked up behind his two front teeth like a pacifier. His long eyelashes hover above pink cheeks and he gazes up at her while she sings to him in a quavering voice and pats his back with crooked fingers. And her hands, twisted and spotty, are beautiful.

They reach out with unconditional love and offer quiet strength to weary souls. They are grown soft as velvet, like the pages of her Bible that have become thin and silky from a lifetime of reading and running her fingers down the promises listed there. I hope my hands look just like hers one day.

THE BOXERS

Never mess with a woman who is thirty-three weeks pregnant.

Normally, I am a levelheaded person. I take life in stride and deal with it. I laugh a lot. I sing to get rid of stress. Someone even once said my spirit was an oasis. I am generally pretty calm.

But my third pregnancy was a whole different ball of wax.

Those few last weeks leading up to delivering my son, Benjamin, were like nothing else. I was huge and swollen. By that stage, I had all of the gentle grace of an African bush elephant. My emotions were wildly skewed. My nose was flattened and spread halfway across my face. I had gestational diabetes and had to give myself insulin three times a day and check my sugar levels every other hour. I longed desperately to plant my face into piles of spaghetti and cheesecake, but had to make do with lettuce and other low-carb proteins. The only shoes that fit me were work boots, tennis shoes and flip flops.

Benjamin was a big baby, and my stomach hung low to the ground. People stared me with horrified sympathy and said, "Oh goodness, honey! How much longer? You look terrible. Oh dear."

One woman even had the intestinal fortitude to walk around behind me to inspect. She tilted her head to the side, put her hand on her waist and remarked, "My goodness. You have ballast butt."

I was confused and asked her to clarify.

"Oh," she said, brimming with tact and wisdom, "That's when your backside becomes so wide that it balances out your big stomach in front."

She will never know how close she came to being thrown to the ground and sat upon.

Our next door neighbors had two beautiful boxers. They enjoyed barking and destroying things. I could glance out of my upstairs window where I worked and see down into the neighbors' backyard. They chained their dogs to a tree during the day, right next to our fence, and provided no shelter for them.

Several times the dogs chewed through our fence and dug holes underneath to get into our yard. We asked the neighbors to fix the damage. They acted puzzled and wondered aloud if our tiny poodle might have possibly chewed the 2-foot holes in the fence. I blocked up the broken fence areas and plugged the holes.

It came to a head finally when the female boxer chewed through again, came into our yard and broke through our back fence to go fight with the dogs that belonged to the neighbors behind us.

The neighbor behind us called the police and confronted the owners of the boxers. Their solution was to lean some old plywood against the fence and call it a day. I was distressed at the ugliness of the back yard, but in my late stage of pregnancy, conditions were not optimal for me to be standing on a ladder doing construction. The repairs had to be delayed and the holes remained.

It was a very rainy, wet, 30-degree day. Shane was occupied downstairs. I was upstairs in my pajamas, with my hair in a knot on top of my head, working at the computer.

One of the boxers chewed through again, still on her chain. She became stuck and wrapped around a tree inside of our yard. She wailed pathetic howls in the rain and I could see her from my upstairs window, struggling to break free.

I do not like big dogs. They scare me. I called downstairs several times, asking Shane to take the dog back to the neighbor's yard. I did not want our other neighbor to call the police again or for the dog to die on our property by hanging or choking. I waited and continued to work. There was no response from Shane.

Something had to be done. I was frustrated and my pregnancy-laden emotions were reaching a boiling point.

After twenty minutes of fruitless waiting and increasing sounds from the panicked dog, I stomped downstairs in my pajamas and floppy tennis shoes. I grabbed a broom to fend off any canine attacks and charged outside into the pouring rain.

I was fearful that the dog would try to bite me when I got close, so I decided to try to act like the alpha dog in the situation. I do not normally make an everyday practice of trying to growl like a wild animal, but that day I did try to make a roaring sound as I hurtled toward her, stomach bouncing, waving my broom in front of me. She cowered, began to whimper and tucked her tail. Score one for the pregnant lady.

Shane came to observe the show from the safety of the back door. I think that was what really set me off, looking up to see him standing there, barefoot, silently watching me and scratching his stomach. I hissed at him to shut the door and go away if he was just going to stand there and not help.

The dog and her chain were already tangled up in a large prickly tree limb and one of the children's bicycles. It was miserable outside. I shook with cold and my teeth chattered as I detangled the dog. My frustration had reached its pinnacle, and I felt that it was a good time to throw something. The bicycle and the tree limb sailed across the yard.

I looked up and saw Shane peeking through the curtain again. I bared my teeth at him and he flicked the curtain back into place. I could still see his nose pressed through the fabric as he watched me from inside.

I finally got the dog unhooked from her restraints. She flew into the air like a loaded spring and pulled me upward with her. I held onto her collar for dear life as we went galloping across the muddy yard and I tried to stay upright as my soaking wet pajamas tried to slide off.

We came flying through the front gate as I held onto the dog with one hand and held up my pajama waist with the other. Ms. Boxer dragged me across the front yard. My posture was swiftly moving into a precarious horizontal slant. My head tilted back towards the gray sky above, hair flopping madly, as my tennis shoes pistoned behind me in large circles in the air and we continued to hurtle full steam ahead through the rain.

My breath began to shorten and I started having contractions. At that point I mentally came to earth and had the rare logical thought that this was a dangerous undertaking both for my unborn child and me. The dog could disappear forever, for all I cared. I also realized that all of our neighbors could see me in my rain-soaked clothing, looking insane. As I considered these points, the dog pulled loose from me and raced down the street. I am sure she was probably as terrified of me as I was of her.

I stood there in the rain, hunched over with my hands on my knees, shoulders heaving, and watched her disappear around the corner. I was drenched to the skin and my hair was matted to my face, creating little pathways for the rain to trickle down onto my nose and chin. I sobbed for a moment, feeling terribly sorry for myself, and then wiped my nose with the back of my arm. I trudged to the back yard to retrieve my broom before I went back inside, looking like a drowned rat.

It was warm and cozy in the house. My loving husband, who has borne patiently with my faults and failures through the years, was sitting on the couch reading a book. He glanced up and gently said, "What's the matter, honey?"

I stood there looking at him and trembled with my fists clenched.

My response came out as a snarl, "Honey, if you can't tell what's wrong by now, don't even bother asking."

I threw my broom in his direction and waddled up the stairs to dry off and return to work. My angry heart rate slowly returned to normal, and Shane wisely chose to stay away from me for several hours.

Insanity is not an appealing attribute for a lady, but it is a fact of life that episodes of violent irrationality will occur during those long months of pregnancy. Thankfully, those incidents calmed down once Benjamin arrived by Caesarean section.

The day prior to his birth fell on a Sunday. Shane was preaching out of town and I had to take care of the service at our own church. I wore my high heels and played the piano and led worship, then went home and hosted Gage's Spiderman-themed birthday party for thirty people. I was so tired that I could have happily crawled under the dining room table and slept for a week.

Shane returned home just in time to see Gage blow out his candles and open his gifts. I raced around like a robot, cleaning up and thanking everyone for coming. Finally, the guests left and I collapsed into a chair.

At 4:00 a.m. the next morning, Shane and I made our way to the hospital. The air was damp with fog and the road was icy. I was exhausted and ready to hold my new baby. We checked in and the nurse prepped me for surgery.

I told Shane goodbye and was wheeled into the operating room. I felt cold panic as I leaned forward for the spinal block. The anesthesiologist was in a bad mood as she inserted the needle. I felt hot pain down to my toes. She dropped a vial of the medicine on the floor, swore loudly and said, "You're just going to have to lean over further."

With a belly the size of an ottoman, I hunched forward even more, lost my balance and almost fell off of the table.

She laid the broken shards of the vial on a

tray next to my bed and tried again. I shut my eyes and prayed for peace through several moments of brilliant pain. She finally finished the spinal block and began to hum.

"Okay, dear. Here we are. Let's move you to another table. 1...2...3. Let's go."

I felt like a whale caught in a net as she counted down, preparing to roll me over. The hospital staff transferred me to the next operating table and I quickly lost feeling from my ribs down.

As I lay there, I began to feel a pleasant buzz. The medication was finally taking effect. I was warm again. Life was good. I could not feel a thing. I looked over and saw Shane floating in the air next to me. I grinned stupidly at him. "Like my hairnet?"

"Yeah, babe. You look hot." He smiled at me and kissed my hand. "We're about to see Benjamin."

The doctors came in and began the surgery. I stared up at the bright lights above me and smelled cauterizing flesh. It seemed like only seconds before the room exploded with, "Well, would you look at that! He's huge. How much do you think he weighs?"

The doctor carried around my 18-wheeler

of a boy and held him up so I could see him. "Look at that," he exclaimed, "I can't believe it. You have an ox here. He weighs – let me see – 11 pounds, 7 ounces!"

I grinned up at a serene bundle who looked nothing like a newborn child. "Hey, munchkin. You're beautiful."

He gazed around at everyone with deep blue eyes and we all fell in love. He never cried until they gave him a bath.

A few hours later, with a face still itching from morphine, I finally held my fat baby in my arms and inhaled in his lotioned scent. He nuzzled close and stared up into my eyes as he nursed.

I pulled out my cell phone and snapped Benjamin's photo. In true drugged form, I updated my Facebook page with a typo-ridden status. I believed at that moment that it was a statement of pure brilliance:

> *"and it came to pass that the days were accomomplished that she should be devivered. And she brought forth her third-hour manchild & laid him in her husband's arms. because she was numb from the rib cage to her toes."*

And the moments of crazed desperation, the leaps and dives of emotion, the pain of surgery, they were all worth it, just to hold that tiny creature for the first time.

Devon and Gage entered the hospital room and stood at the foot of the bed. "Look, mom!" Gage said, "I've just eaten a bunch of rice. I'm growing strong and filthy!"

Gage flexed his muscles and his little chest poked out as he inspected his new brother. Devon rested her head on my shoulder. I caught her eye and we shared a silent grin together over Gage's choice of words. Then I took a deep breath, leaned back and smiled at the people surrounding my bed, and closed my eyes.

THE PLAGUES

From ghoulies and ghosties
And long-leggedy beasties
And things that go bump in the night,
Good Lord, deliver us!
-Traditional Scottish Prayer

Warning: The reading of this chapter may cause extreme nausea.

It would be wonderful to say it was just a nightmare and I woke up the next morning with a creepy feeling and no harm done. That, however, was not the case. Just writing this chapter caused me to gag and feel itchy and sadly mortified all over again.

All of my life I have lived in a bug-free home. Ants and flies have ventured in when a window or door was left open, but they were always quickly killed off. I do not even know what a bedbug looks like. I scrub and clean until my knuckles are red. My children have never had lice.

After a long and happy life without bugs, however, we became the involuntary victims of an infestation in our home several years ago.

By sight alone now, I can quickly identify three of the most common types of cockroaches.

The first kind is the American cockroach. This may be what you see in your mind's eye when you think "cockroach". It is commonly known as a water bug or a palmetto. It is huge, about two inches long. Its dark brown exoskeleton is like a tiny suit of impenetrable armor. It will not crunch underfoot. You can hammer it with a family Bible and run over it with a truck, and it will still run around at the speed of light.

We never saw this kind of bug except when it rained. Then one lone visitor would sneak into the house, dart up the wall and skitter across the ceiling. The kids and I would scream and Shane would laugh. Then it would disappear until the next downpour.

My mother was visited by such a water bug as she worked at our computer one peaceful, drizzly day. I sat across the room on a couch and watched her calm demeanor evaporate as she suddenly screeched like a banshee and her eyes bulged out. She kicked out her leg and lunged out of her chair. She began to dance frantically around, letting out an occasional war whoop, flapping her arms up and down and clutching at her skirt. I laid back and shook with helpless laughter as she continued to yell and tried to shake off the long scratchy-legged critter that had come in out of the rain and decided to run up her leg.

Those kinds of instances I can handle, especially when I am the observer and not the participant.

The other two species, though, are the ones that traumatized me.

The brown-banded cockroach is a small brown bug. It has light colored bands highlighted on its wings. It likes to spend its days living inside of tiny cracks. It prefers warm, dry locations and especially likes electronic equipment and refrigerator housings. It comes out at night to search for food, and only occasionally during the day. It could win races for its supernatural speed.

The German cockroach is a small, half-inch pest who prefers to live close to moisture and food. It likes to eat just about anything, whether in a bathroom or a kitchen. It is a tough creature to eliminate because of its ability to lay

45 eggs at a time.

Both of these types squash easily, if you can catch them before they hit their "0-to-60-in-4-seconds" mode.

After launching our new church, we had a sudden influx of people asking for money, food and clothing. There were all kinds of needs. It just came with the territory.

One man who visited the church several times told Shane that he was being evicted and just needed somewhere to put his things for a few weeks. Shane agreed to store the man's belongings at our house. I came home one day and discovered six garbage bags of clothing, a very dirty old recliner, and some bins of personal belongings stacked in our garage. I bit my tongue and said nothing. In my innocence, it never occurred to me to wonder about someone else's hygiene habits. I occasionally asked Shane when his friend's things would be picked up, but never received a response.

Several weeks later, I was cleaning the kitchen and saw a tiny brown bug with antennae sneaking up the wall in the kitchen. I pounced on it, but it was too quick for me and raced out of my reach. I realized that it was a roach and was immediately panicked and nauseated. I had never seen a small roach before. I had heard a few times that if one roach can be seen out in the open, there are usually hundreds more hiding in the walls.

I immediately went to the store and bought Raid, sprayed down the house, and scrubbed down the walls, furniture and fixtures all night. No bugs were spotted again for several days. I never thought to examine the man's belongings which sat abandoned in our garage.

Shane is a tenderhearted soul. He weeps with those who are weeping. He loves to give to the needy and the downtrodden. It makes him happy to be able to help others. He approached me a few weeks later and asked if I would be open to letting a married couple stay at our house for a few weeks while they searched for another apartment and new jobs. I was nursing a four-month-old baby, and my maternal tendencies were still elevated, so I agreed.

Jack and Martha moved in several days later. Piles of their belongings went into the garage. More items, including clothing and a large, empty fish tank, went into Gage's bedroom upstairs. Gage moved into our bedroom, because it was only temporary – or so we thought.

That first night we stood in the kitchen after showing our guests through the house. Martha stood next to me looking around and then said, "I wanna go look through your closet and find me some shoes."

I wondered to myself why all of the shoes that she owned were now insufficient.

"What size do you wear?" I said.

"Ten."

"I wear 8-1/2. I don't think mine will fit you, but you're welcome to try," I said.

"Naw," she shook her head. "Never mind," she said and shuffled away.

The bug population suddenly increased when our guests moved in. I constantly asked our guests to make sure to take out the trash and clean up after themselves, but my exhortations went ignored. The bugs began to exhibit brazenness and sauntered around the house in broad daylight, as if daring me to try to kill them. At night, they would scatter in droves when the lights came on in the kitchen, little brown dots fleeing across the surface of the counters and walls. I became frantic and called the exterminator.

The exterminator came out four times in one week, but the infestation was overpowering. I could look down at the trash can to see roaches grazing on food that had been thrown out. Underneath the bathroom sink, bugs crept

around happily in their warm, dark home.
When the toilet lid was raised, a bug or two
would dart out from under the edge and run for
cover. When I cooked dinner, bugs would
suddenly begin crawling up the wall from behind
the stove, awakened by the heat.

There was an ever-present knot of nausea
in my stomach over our state of affairs. I was too
mortified to approach anyone outside of the
situation for advice.

A few weeks turned into a month, and still
our guests stayed, without any movement
towards obtaining jobs. I was growing weary of
constantly being polite in my own home, where
nothing was being contributed for our extra
utility costs or groceries. When I went grocery
shopping, Martha threw items into the cart with
abandon, never asking, and when I removed
them, there would be an angry silence.

The house was always a mess when I
arrived home from work. I would immediately
cook dinner and get the children bathed and
ready for bed. Once they were asleep, I worked
my second job online, cleaned house for several
hours and then collapsed into bed.

The refrigerator began to take on a life of
its own. The drawers were filled with tight little
parcels of foreign leftovers packed in wadded tin
foil balls that were "being saved for later", a bite

of hot dog, two spoons of macaroni, a slice of old tomato.

Jack came in one day from the garage. "Well," he said, "I know where them bugs are coming from. There's an old recliner in the garage and it's just full of 'em."

I gagged and had a frantic conversation with Shane. Within the hour, the old recliner found a new home on a quiet roadside several miles out in the country. But the bugs continued to multiply at the house. I scrubbed and cleaned harder than ever, with tears of anger running down my face.

After cleaning and disinfecting every day, I would lie awake in bed at night, praying and sobbing with desperate frustration and absolute embarrassment.

"God, please kill these bugs. I can't live like this. I've done everything I can." Devon was just as distraught, and cried along with me.

We went out of town one weekend to have some family time to ourselves and get away from the chaos. When we returned, laid out on our front porch was a new hand-knotted wool rug that I was saving to put in Shane's office. It was being used as a doormat and was soaked with rain and mud.

Our guests proudly led us into the garage and gestured around. My feet started to tingle. They had "cleaned" for us by moving all of our belongings into one corner of the garage, tightly stacked in a pile from floor to ceiling. I stared at the mountain and wondered how on earth I would ever get it sorted out.

Martha turned to me. "Oh," she said, "We did up your dining room for you, too."

I could not speak. My heart was thumping in my chest by the time we got to the dining room.

It had been redecorated.

The furniture was moved around. The huge wooden carved picture frame with silver leaf that I loved and had leaned against the wall as a decorative accent was gone. I later discovered it pulled apart in multiple pieces and placed in the garage.

Old, crumbling corsages and treasures from my childhood that our guests had found in storage boxes were placed carefully at intervals around the room and lined the windowsills. I looked in quiet alarm at the framed photos of our children that had been laid face-down on the piano.

I gazed up with wide open mouth and

beheld the crowning glory. Around our dining room hung small pictures in colorful plastic frames from my teenage years. Our guests had decided to nail them all high up on the walls at different spots, about ten inches from the ceiling.

There were places in the walls where the arrangement of the photos obviously had not met with the decorators' satisfaction. Several turns with the hammer and nails had been taken before the pictures finally passed muster, because multiple empty nail holes abounded.

The couple stood there with big grins, hands clasped together, waiting for my deep gratitude.

I was speechless for several moments as I gazed around. I finally managed to say, "Oh....wow. You have been working hard."

I was heartsick inside. My beautiful home was turning upside down. I did not have the heart to take down the pictures yet. I could not find a thing in our garage without taking apart the ceiling-high mass of heaped items.

We reached the three-month mark of our guests' stay and still they made no move to find jobs or their own residence. There was no relief in sight. Although we were providing their shelter, food and utilities, they began to complain about things they believed we were doing wrong, and how they felt they were being treated unfairly.

Several times, we opened our bedroom door to discover them standing outside, listening to our conversations. There was no privacy in our own home. We tiptoed around, trying not to offend our guests. Tension was growing. And I lived with a dark cloud of horror hanging over me because of the bugs.

Jack came home drunk several nights in a row and began acting belligerent. I knew that it was only a matter of time before he hauled off and hurt one of us or our children, and I asked Shane to please tell the couple that they needed to leave. I kept all of the children in our bedroom at night with the door locked.

Several days passed and still they stayed. I came in to talk to Shane and pleaded with him. "They have to leave."

"I'll tell them they have to be gone in two weeks," he said.

"By the end of this week," I said.

"But, babe, they have nowhere to go."

"They are adults," I said. "They survived before they came into our house. We barely have enough money to feed our own children, let alone two people who are well able to find jobs and support themselves, and they will find another place. Trust me."

His shoulders slumped and he sighed. "Okay. I just don't want them to be upset."

Little red flashes of light went off behind my eyes. I shut my mouth and refrained from saying things that would have added more strain to an already uptight situation.

After everyone else was in bed that night, I came downstairs to clean yet again. I placed a lamp next to the front door to take the next morning to decorate my office. It was tall, with a beautiful black wood base and grayish-green silk shade.

I went into the kitchen. Next to the stove was a Keurig coffee maker. It was Shane's Christmas present from my parents. It brought him no end of pride and joy. He liked to show it off for company. I needed to stay awake for several hours, so I grasped the handle and opened the top of the coffeemaker to insert a K-cup.

Five or six little brown roaches plopped out and fell onto the countertop, where they immediately scuttled out of my reach. I screamed and jumped back. The K-cup flew wildly across the room somewhere behind me. I stood there and stared at the coffeemaker, overwhelmed with rage at the bugs and the people that had overtaken my house.

Out of the corner of my eye, I noticed something coming out from under the coffeemaker and tilted it sideways. A roach was emerging out of a screw hole. I emptied the water bin and turned the machine upside down. I took the bottom off and inspected the motor inside. It was warm and cozy. It was crawling with a layer of roaches, moving lazily through the inner workings of the machine.

That was enough. I was done. I grabbed a trash bag, flung the entire piece of machinery into it and tied the bag into a tight knot. I set it outside on the front porch to wait until morning, and then lay down on the couch and cried. I did not care whether or not our house guests heard me. I had had it. I went upstairs and tried to sleep.

Before the sun was even up the next morning, we were awakened by a loud knock on our bedroom door.

"'Scuse me!" Jack hollered out, "We seen the coffee machine sitting out on the front porch. Are y'all throwing it away? 'Cause we want it!"

I groaned and looked over at Shane, who

was still unaware of the situation. "I'm so sorry, hon," I whispered. "I had to throw away your coffeemaker."

His face crumpled as he sat up. "What? Why?"

"It was full of roaches, even inside the motor." I could feel my lip quivering as angry tears began to surface again.

His face was a picture of sad disgust. He shook his head as he crawled out of bed and went to answer the door. I heard my tenderhearted husband outside the bedroom. "I'm sorry, Jack. The coffeemaker is not coming back inside this house. Leave it alone."

"Oh. Well." was the man's response. There was a moment of silence, and then, "How 'bout that lamp sitting there by the door? Is that broke too? 'Cause we want it. We can fix it."

"No. No. The lamp's working fine. That's my wife's. She is taking it to her office."

"Well, then. Huh." Jack's voice faded as he walked back into their bedroom and informed Martha of the current state of affairs.

I was weary of having our personal belongings inspected and handled as if our house was a thrift shop. We had hardly any food left. I was afraid for our personal safety. The bugs were an added piece of tragedy to the mix. Our home was no longer a sanctuary of quiet rest and had not been for a long time.

Another week passed and still our house was occupied. I came home from work that Friday afternoon. Jack and Martha were out. Lying on the counter in the children's bathroom was a portable man's urinal that had been left there by one of the guests. It was old and dirty and lined with a thick yellow crust. I retched and backed out of the bathroom, not even wanting to think about why it was there.

The tipping point had been reached. Mama Bear realized that she would have to take drastic measures, because things were never going to change otherwise.

I took a deep breath and went downstairs to sit on the couch next to my husband. "Hon, there's something you need to see in the kid's bathroom upstairs. I'm not touching it. I'm going to visit my mom tonight, okay?"

I said it with calmness, even though my insides were quaking.

"Cool," he said, "Have fun. You need the break."

"Come on, kids! We're going to go see

Nana!" I said.

The kids jumped up and down and yelled happy yells. A trip to Nana's house at the ranch was the pinnacle of fun. We packed our backpacks and I threw in some extra clothes. We kissed Shane goodbye and headed down the road. An hour down the road, I called my mother. I updated her on the situation and asked, "Is it okay if we stay for a little while? It's not safe at home anymore, and I'm not going back until they're gone."

Grandmother Bear agreed to let us stay and hung up growling.

When I got off the phone, Gage tapped me on the shoulder. "Mamma? When are we coming back?"

"We're taking a little vacation, baby, while Jack and Martha move out. We'll be back when they're gone, okay?"

"Yay! We're going on vacation!" He was ecstatic.

We arrived at the ranch at sundown and stepped into my parent's serene home. It was cool and dark and pristine inside. I wanted to lie down and sleep for a month. I gave my mother a grateful smile. "Thanks for letting us stay."

That evening, I called Shane. Gage asked to talk to him.

"Hi, Daddy!" he said, "We're having fun! Thanks for letting us go on vacation!"

I could hear Shane's voice on the other end, "What do you mean, buddy?"

"Mamma said we get to stay here 'til Jack and Martha leave! Thanks, Daddy!"

"Hey, buddy. Let me talk to Mamma."
My stomach dropped. The gig was up. I hated confrontations.

"Okay, here she is. I love you, Daddy!"

"Love you too, Gage."

I put the phone to my ear. "Hello."

"What's going on, Randa?" He said my name. I knew he was serious.

"Oh, we're just here at the ranch," I said.

"You're not coming back right now?"

My insides were quivering, and my response came out as a wavering question. "Not until they're gone?"

There was a long silence on the other end of the line. "You're serious?"

"Yes, I am. I promise I'm not trying to be mean. It's just that the kids have to be safe, and I'm going to make sure that happens."

More silence, and then a tired voice. "Okay. They'll be gone tomorrow. I'll let you know when they're out."

"Thank you," I felt my voice starting to crack with tears. "I love you. I'll talk to you soon."

"Love you too, hon. I really do," he said.

I clicked off the phone and sat back against the sofa with my eyes closed. Relief started to seep through me. It had been a long time arriving, but the ordeal was finally coming to an end.

ANY GIVEN SUNDAY

We were awakened at 6:00 a.m. that Sunday morning by the youth pastor who had gone up to the church early to finish preparing his sermon. When he arrived at the church, he discovered rags stuffed down in the janitor's closet sink. The water was turned on full blast. It had been on all night and the church was flooded. We jumped up, threw on the first clothing we could find, loaded the children into the truck, and drove like demons to the church.

When we walked in, the downstairs was flooded with standing water several inches deep. The entire left side of the church downstairs was soaked, including half of the sanctuary, the church offices and several other rooms. We called a commercial water extraction company, who arrived quickly, threw open the doors and set up giant fans and dehumidifiers throughout the sanctuary.

Shane's office, which was located just next
door to the janitor's closet, got the brunt of it.
His beautiful handmade desk was standing in
water. His sermon notes were soaked. We
removed all of the furniture from his office,
pulled up all of the carpet, and set his desk up
on concrete blocks. We filed a police report and
prayed that the damage would be covered by
insurance.

Three hours later, most of the water was
vacuumed up, but the carpets were still soaked.
Someone tapped me on the shoulder, and I
turned around to see a stark naked Gage being
held up for inspection by a concerned church
member. They notified me that my two-year-old
son had stripped down and had been standing at
the altar in his birthday suit for several minutes,
watching the huge fans in action.

I recovered articles of my son's clothing
that were scattered around the front of the
church and began to dress him again in the
restroom. I looked in the mirror and realized
my eyes were wild and my face was bright red
from heavy physical activity. My curly hair was
sticking up all over my head. I looked like a hag
and smelled like a goat from all of the furniture
moving.

I glanced down and saw that my black
sandals had gotten wet from wading through

water for the past few hours, and my feet were dyed in various shades of black from toe to ankle. I crouched in the ladies bathroom sink and scrubbed with paper towels and hand soap. It did nothing to remove the stains on my feet. I smoothed down my hair as best as I could and sprayed it. It was time for church and too late to do anything more. The preacher's wife marched up to the choir loft on mottled feet that appeared to be severely frostbitten.

Morning worship service began. The music lessened the effect of the roaring machines, but it still sounded like we were at an air show. People stood around with their mouths hanging open and stared at the novelty of the huge dehumidifiers and vacuums.

I stood singing in the front row of the choir and shivered as I felt a cold draft somewhere around my midsection. I reached down and saw that my shirt had ridden up. My cheeks turned crimson and my toes tingled. I realized that five hundred people had just witnessed my bright white stomach shining like a beacon. There was nothing I could do but casually smooth down my shirt and keep singing. I wished that I could go home and crawl under the covers for several days.

Fast forward to the afternoon. We attended a party out in the country. I have a faint recollection of staring around the room with a plate in my hand, but little else. I was already exhausted from the morning drama.

When we left the party, I stumbled behind Shane in a half-awake stupor, carrying a snoring Gage. There was a seven-inch-thick oak tree branch with the knob on the end just hanging there in mid-air, right in our path. Shane quietly evaded the branch and went on. In my oblivion, I plowed into the branch with the full force of my momentum. My forehead and right eye took a direct hit.

Stars began shooting around my peripheral vision before I realized what happened. I yelled out in pain and staggered backward. Shane had already walked around to his side of the vehicle and missed the pleasure of seeing me attempt to knock my brains loose. I swayed momentarily and then wobbled my way to the truck. I managed not to drop my son.

My nose was running and my eyes were pouring with involuntary tears when I crawled into the front seat, holding my head. Shane glanced over at me and noticed the damage.

"Did you hurt yourself on that branch?" he asked with gentle concern.

"Oh no," I sniffled, "It actually felt very pleasant. Almost like a massage."

We headed to the hospital to visit a sick church member. I tried to rest on the way, and my head lolled back and forth, throbbing. A large goose egg was beginning to puff up above my right eyebrow. There was an angry red scrape of a ring around my eye.

In my state of agony, I thought it best not to scare any parishioners, so I stayed in the truck with the children while Shane went inside the hospital. They fought in the back seat for thirty minutes and pelted each other with balloons while I held my hands over my ears and tried to ignore the migraine.

By the time the hospital visit was over, it was time to head back to the evening service. I endured the next several hours of church with blurred vision and pounding cranium. My right eye kept squinting, pouring tears and closing shut from intense pain.

During a quiet portion of the sermon, Gage looked over at me for a moment and then grinned. As I smiled back at him, he hopped out of his chair and ran past me down the aisle. I jumped up, cast aside my dignity and tried to forget that everyone was watching me as I charged down the aisle after my two-year-old. He looked over his shoulder, saw me coming, and began to yell out an urgent, "Help! Help!" with imploring gestures at anyone who would look at him.

Mid-gallop I wondered again to myself why I always felt like an awkward elephant moving in slow motion every time I tried to snag a small running child. As he rounded the corner at the back of the sanctuary, I finally caught him and deposited him in the nursery for the duration of the service.

By the end of the church service, I was so frazzled that I looked like I had been walking through a wind tunnel. My injured right eye was gummed shut. My hair gel had stopped working hours ago and fuzzy curls were sticking up all over my head again. Without fail, whenever my hair sticks up, people ask me how I have been doing lately and if I am going through something. This night was no exception.

One man walked up next to me with his head cocked to the side and worry on his face. He simply patted my arm without a word as he shook his head with sympathy. A few minutes later, a lady sat down next to me and considered my face for a moment.

"Oh, honey," she finally said, "I've HAAAAD you on my mind."

I stared at her through my good eye and waited silently for her continue.

"But everything's going to be okay." She nodded slowly.

"Yes...." She gazed deep into my eyes like a seer. "You're here.... Mm hmm.... For such a time as this."

"HUH?"

I gazed at her for a moment, hoping that I had not spoken aloud. She widened her eyes as she waited for my ecstatic reply. I could not come up with any intelligent-sounding response.

"I've been praying for you," she said, still searching my expression.

That one I could answer. I gave her a lopsided grateful smile and thanked her with a hug. She stood and then invaded my personal space by patting my hair down against my skull. I was too tired to stop her. She walked away, satisfied that her job was done.

It was later that night when Shane and I turned off all the lights and left the building. As we began to buckle the children into their car seats, I decided to stop trying to be perfect. I realized that sometimes life decides to pull out all of the stops, and you just have to roll with it and keep doing your best.

I finished out that day looking a bit worse for wear. I could barely see, but my family was together, they loved me, and we were healthy and safe. They didn't care if their mamma had a shiner and bad hair. They never commented on my black feet. These little people and their daddy were the ones who mattered most to me. Shane reached over and laid his hand on my shoulder. I let out a sigh and rested my closed eyes against his hand. And as we drove home in the quiet darkness, I resolved to stop worrying about everyone else.

ONE WILD NATIVITY

Christmas time rolled down upon us with the force of a landslide that year. We were still holding church services in a hotel ballroom. Our options and funds for a children's Christmas play were limited, and I could not find anything that fit our budget. So I wrote it myself. I never thought corralling ten children (three of whom were mine) could be so difficult, or that play practice would be such an exercise in futility. In the end it turned out beautifully.

Wearing thrift store sheets and pillowcases with the armholes cut out, our tiny actors looked like they stepped out of ancient Bible times. At the dollar store we found a classical Christmas music CD and some plastic jewels for the wise men.

A donated backdrop with a hand-painted hillside scene, and some free crowns from

Burger King completed our scavenging. With only $4.00 spent on the CD and jewels, I felt pretty happy.

The big day arrived and the children milled around in their finery. I was hot and frazzled after ten minutes. Our Angel Gabriel failed to appear at dress rehearsal. He tearfully explained over the phone that his mother had a hangover and refused to let him leave the house. Time for Plan B.

"Shane? Can you please be my Gabriel instead of the narrator? Since my parents are visiting, I could ask my dad to narrate." I pleaded with him while sweat ran down my back. "I can wrap you up in a bigger sheet. See? Like this."

A look of longsuffering fell over Shane's face and he agreed to become the Angel. I ran to my father and handed him the script. A few minutes later, everyone was seated and the play began with the tired and sweaty pastor's wife accompanying herself on the keyboard and singing "Mary, Did You Know."

The mellow brass and soft strings from the Christmas CD slowly faded in and the music was left on for the duration of the play for ambiance. A hush fell and all eyes were on center stage where a little primitive crate rested, full of straw.

The narrator began.

"Listen, children. Listen to the prophecy of old! The people that walked in darkness have seen a great light. They that dwell in the land of the shadow of death, upon them hath the light shined. For unto us a child is born, unto us a son is given. And the government shall be upon his shoulder: and his name shall be called Wonderful, Counselor, the mighty God, the everlasting Father, the prince of peace. Of the increase of his government and in peace there shall be no end. Upon the throne of David and upon his kingdom to order it and to establish it with judgment and with justice from henceforth even forever. The zeal of the Lord of hosts will perform this."

Devon, a very tall Mary-With-An-Attitude, sneaked in from the side and plopped down on a chair facing the audience, trying to look peaceful. Her headgear was askew and her studied expression appeared more vacant than serene.

The narrator continued, "And in the sixth month the angel Gabriel was sent from God unto a city of Galilee named Nazareth to a virgin espoused to a man whose name was Joseph of the house of David and the virgin's name was Mary."

Shane, my pinch-hitter Gabriel, tiptoed in

from the right, draped in a billowing white sheet. He flapped his arms madly up and down like an insane pelican and crept up behind the unsuspecting Mary, dancing on his toes with a devious grin. Ready to deliver his shocking annunciation, he leaned forward.

The narrator cleared his voice, "And the angel came into unto her and said--"

"HAAAAILLL MARY!" Gabriel roared into Mary's tender ear.

"THELORDISWITHYOU!"

Mary screeched, fell off her chair in mock fright and cowered, covering her eyes. Gabriel pointed down at Mary.

"YOU are highly favored and blessed among women," he said.

Mary scooted backward on her behind and held up her hand to ward him off. "You stay back! Who are you and why are you saying these things to me?"

Gabriel shook his head. "Don't be scared, Mary. You've found favor with God. You are going to have a baby!"

"Ex-CUSE me?" Mary managed to pull off the perfect combination of confusion and righteous indignation."

"A BABY," Gabriel was beginning to lose his patience. "You know, one of those little things that cries and eats and gets dirty diapers."

"HOLY. Moley." Mary hunched over for a moment and stared off into space.

Gabriel gave a nonchalant shrug. "Yeah. He'll be the son of the most high and all that. And of his kingdom there shall be no end."

Mary looked up at Gabriel.

"Um, like how is this supposed to happen? I'm, like, not even married yet? Totally uncool, especially in these Biblical times."

"Oh yes." Gabriel nodded, "Funny you should mention that. That's the best part. The Holy Ghost will come over you and the power of the highest will overshadow you. No biggie. Nothing's impossible with God."

Mary pursed her lips and hitched her shoulders.

"Well, if you say so, let it be done." She stood up, put her hands on her hips and struck a pose with her lips pursed out.

"Check me out, yo. I'm the handmaiden

of the Lord."

Gabriel and Mary exited.

Joseph, a tiny 5-year-old boy with freckles, reddish-brown curls and sparkling eyes, ran in and threw himself down on the floor, pretending to be asleep.

The narrator waited until Joseph situated himself into a position of optimal slumber, then said, "Now, when Joseph found out, being a just man and not willing to make her a public example, he was minded to put her away privately. But while he thought on those things, the angel of the Lord appeared unto him in a dream."

Gabriel flapped and circled his way back to the stage and tapped Joseph on the shoulder. "Joseph, wake up!"

Joseph wriggled his foot and kept his eyes closed, "Ugh. I'm asleep," he mumbled with an impish grin, "Leave me 'lone."

Gabriel shook him harder. "Joseph! Joseph, don't be afraid to marry Mary."

Joseph sat up, yawned, and then crossed his arms in defiance. "But she's having a BABY!" he complained, "And we're NOT even MARRIED!"

Joseph looked away from Gabriel and flashed a huge smile around the audience, waving at his mother.

Gabriel was exasperated. "Joseph! The baby she's carrying is by the Holy Ghost. And she will have the baby and you will call his name Jesus because he will save his people from their sin."

Joseph could not keep the wicked grin from covering his face again as he gave the audience one more peek, then huffed and crossed his arms.

"Okay, FINE."

Joseph and Gabriel exited the stage and Joseph ran to the back of the room where Mary was waiting for him. Together Joseph and Mary walked slowly down the aisle.

Joseph was a good two feet shorter than Mary, who hobbled on painful feet. The pillow stuffed under her robe kept trying to fall out, so she grabbed her lopsided baby belly and carried it under her left arm for the rest of the way like a rolled up sleeping bag. She stumbled, very tired, and Joseph repeatedly looked up at her with an anxious expression.

The narrator's voice grew deeper. "And it

came to pass in those days that there went out a decree from Cesar Augustus that all the world should be taxed. And all went to be taxed, everyone into his own city. And Joseph also went up from Galilea out of the city of Nazareth into Judea unto the city of David which is called Bethlehem because the house and lineage of David, to be taxed with Mary his espoused wife, being great with child."

Joseph cranked his head back, reached up and patted Mary's shoulder. "Almost there, dear. We're almost there."

Mary sighed. "I know, Joseph. I'm just so tired. I feel like this baby could be born any minute."

They reached the end of the aisle as the narrator resumed his story.

"And so it was that while they were there, the days were accomplished that she should be delivered."

Mary pulled the pillow back around to the front and then grabbed at her stomach with exaggerated drama, "Ohhhh! Owwww!!!" she yelled, "The baby's coming. Joseph! I need somewhere to have this baby! NOW!"

Joseph looked up at Mary with his mouth hanging open and then turned to bang frantically on an upended 8-foot-long wooden table which was intended to represent the innkeeper's door.

"Open up! Hurry! We need a room! My wife's about to have a baby!"

The innkeeper poked his head around the side of the table. He shook his head vehemently, looking for all the world like a character from the Mad Hatter's tea party in Alice in Wonderland.

"No ROOOM! No ROOM! Good bye!" The innkeeper disappeared behind the door.

Joseph banged again while Mary stood next to him moaning sadly and holding up her pillow under her robe.

The innkeeper stepped around the door and held out his arms in emphatic resignation, "What now? I TOLD you I don't have any rooms!"

"Sir! We'll take whatever you have," Joseph said, "Please! I beg you--"

Joseph stopped suddenly and then turned to the script prompter with a yell, "What comes next? I forgot."

"The baby's coming," the prompter hissed.

"THE BABY'S COMING!" Joseph
bawled in the innkeeper's face.

The innkeeper scratched his head. "Hang
on. Let me think…"

Mary pressed her hands into the small of
her back and whined, "Ohhhhh, my back. I'd
even be happy for a STABLE right now."

She wriggled her eyebrows at the
innkeeper, desperately hinting.

"Hmmm," said the innkeeper, "Oh! Hey!
I have a stable in the back. It stinks and it's full
of animals, but you're welcome to it."

He led Mary and Joseph a few steps away
to one of the hotel's luggage carts that had been
transformed with black cloth and straw into a
stable of sorts. The tiny manger sat in front of it.

The narrator's voice boomed out. "And
she brought forth her firstborn son and wrapped
him in swaddling clothes and laid him in a
manger because there was no room for them in
the inn."

While the narrator spoke, Mary stepped
behind the stable to drop her pillow, but failed
to completely hide herself before she yanked it
out from under her robe and threw it over her

shoulder onto the floor. The tittering audience began to laugh out loud.

While Joseph carefully spread a small blanket down on top of the straw in the manger, Mary ran to the front row where my mother held a 9-month-old Benjamin.

He wore a diaper covered in soft white cloth and he was snoring loudly. His cheeks were flushed and surrounded with soft blonde curls. He sucked on his bottom lip, dreaming of his next bottle. He was going to be a perfect baby Jesus.

The room grew quiet as Mary carried Jesus back to the manger. The baby's head bobbled back and forth on Mary's shoulder and she grunted from his weight as she laid him down on the straw. He never awakened. Mary and Joseph sat on the edge of the luggage cart and stared down at the pudgy sleeping bundle.

"Mary," Joseph leaned down and poked the baby's shoulder, "Are you sure you didn't wrap him too tight?"

"Oh no." Mary was a firm young mother. "No. That's the way you're supposed to do it. Isn't he beautiful?"

The miniature Joseph gave her an upwards dubious glance. "Um. Sure.... He has lots of

hair. And look at his fingers. They're so little."
He patted Jesus and tilted his own head with a
smile to watch him sleep. The baby was half as
big as Joseph was.

Mary elbowed Joseph and they had a
whispered consultation that could be heard five
rows back. "We're 'sposed to sing now!"

"Huh?" Joseph was oblivious.

"Silent Night! You're 'sposed to sing it
with me!"

"Oh. Okay," Joseph was amenable to the
idea. They stood and sang their version of the
ancient carol in clear, sweet voices.

Silent night, hooooly night
All is calm, all is bright
Round yum virgin
Mother and child
Holy IIIN-fant-SO
Tender and wild
Sleep in heavenly peeaaaace,
Slee-heep in heh—

Both simultaneously took a deep breath,
blew it out, and then continued.

—venly peace

The song ended and the singers looked

down again at the baby. A deep silence wound itself throughout the sanctuary, broken only by an occasional sniffle. The 2,000-year-old story was coming alive once again.

On the other side of the stage in front of the hillside set stood three pintsized shepherds in a huddle, holding their staffs and shading their eyes, as if watching their sheep. Tea towels covered their heads, held in place by large rubber bands. They held long staffs made from wooden closet rods.

The narrator continued in resonant tones. "And there were in the same country shepherds abiding in the fields keeping watch over their flock by night."

The shepherds waited for their cue and began to yell, "Heeere, sheepy! Heeere, sheepy, sheepy, sheepy!"

"And LO," said the narrator, "The angel of the Lord CAAAME upon them."

The Angel Gabriel charged back onto the scene with the force of a rodeo bull, flapping his arms vehemently and whirling in circles.

The narrator roared, "And the glory of the Lord shone round about them and they were SORE afraid!"

The shepherds jumped, screaming like girls. They scrabbled backward and fell down in their haste to get away.

"Aaaaaagh! AAAAAGGGH!!!! Please don't eat us! We don't taste good. We smell like sheep. Try Bethlehem - they taste better over there! AAAAGH!"

"Don't be scared!" shouted Gabriel, "I'm not here to eat you. I have good news. Today, a savior is born in the city of David! It's Christ the Lord! Go now -- you'll know it's him because he's wrapped in swaddling clothes and lying in a manger."

"And SUDDENLY," yelled the narrator, "There was with the angel a multitude of the heavenly host, praising God and saying...."

A hastily assembled angel choir, draped in white with teetering halos, began to flap their arms and holler, "GLORY TO GOD IN THE HIGHEST, AND ON EARTH, PEACE, GOOD WILL TOWARD MEN!" They chanted lustily until shushed by the prompter, and then died away as one small boy chirped out a final, "Good will toward mens!"

The shepherds whispered amongst themselves for a moment and one finally said, "Hey guys, let's go to Bethlehem right now and check it out."

They exited stage left and ran toward the back. In our minds' eyes, we could see them running down an old dusty road against the backdrop of a dark night filled with stars.

The angel choir stayed in position, some picking their noses. One miniature angel yelled that he had to go potty and began dancing in place.

"And they came with haste," said the narrator, "And found Mary and Joseph and the baby lying in a manger."

The shepherds ran en masse back up the middle aisle to kneel before the manger, gasping for breath. "We're not sheep – whew – we didn't get eaten. Where's the baby? We saw angels!"

"Huh?" said Mary. "Shhhhh!!!! The baby's right here, but he's asleep! Don't you dare wake him up."

Joseph sat up straight and tall, the proud little father. "You can look," he said in his high soprano voice, "But DON'T touch."

The shepherds bowed down to the manger with their faces to the ground again and again, up and down with their hands slapping the ground. "Hallelujah! Hallelujah! This is incredible! Wow! Hey -- cute baby!"

As the shepherds continued their adoration of the sleeping Jesus, the narrator began again.

"Now when Jesus was born in Bethlehem of Judea in the days of Herod the king, there came wise men from the east to Jerusalem. And lo, the star which they saw in the east, went before them until it came and stood over where the young child was. And when they saw the star, they rejoiced with great joy."

While the narrator spoke, two of the shepherds jumped up from the manger and sped off toward the back of the sanctuary, where they were quickly transformed into wise men wearing Burger King crowns, jewelry and shiny gold robes made from cheap holiday tablecloths. When the narrator was finished, the wise men entered, stomping loudly down the aisle in a stiff, robotic march, holding their travel bags.

"We. Are. Wise." said Gage as Wise Man 1. He wore glasses and his curly hair peeked out from under his crown. He spoke in a mechanical voice.

"We. Three. Kings. Of. Orient. ARE." said Wise Man 2 in a loud bellow.

As they neared the end of the aisle, Wise Man 3 piped up. "Where-is-the-newborn-king-of-the-JEWS?"

"We have seen his star in the EAST," said Wise Man 1, "So. Cool."

"We've come to worship Him," said Wise Man 2, looking around and pretending not to see the manger directly in front of him. "Where. Is. He?"

"And they came and saw the child with Mary his mother," said the narrator, "and fell down and worshipped him."

Three little wise men took the narrator's words literally, collapsing and wilting to the ground in front of the manger, then bowing down. They stood back up and hopped around in a solemn, expressionless circle, chanting in their robotic voices.

"Hallelujah. Hallelujah. Wow. This is incredible. Hallelujah. Praise God. Yaaayyyy."

Wise Man 3 suddenly stopped hopping, and his dignified composure disappeared. "Hey, we almost forgot the gifts."

The wise men ran to retrieve their gifts from their bags, and then went back down on their knees in front of the manger.

Wise Man 3 looked up at Mary. "We have

treasures for Jesus. See?" He pointed at his comrades.

"I. Have. Gold." said Wise Man 1, holding out a bag of plastic Chuck E. Cheese tokens.

"This is Frank in Tents." Said Wise Man 2, handing over a 2-foot tall decorative finial that had been requisitioned from someone's living room. The top of the finial had already cracked off in transit from the back of the sanctuary to the front of the manger.

Wise Man 3 piped up. "I. Have. Mirth." he said in earnest as he placed an ornate bowl in Mary's hands. Laughter spilled out from the audience behind him and he looked back, puzzled at the response.

Wise Man 1 was not to be outdone. "Keep out of reach of children," he shouted. "Subject to availability. Tax, title and license not included."

Mary was gracious. "Oh, thank you, wise men. That's very kind of you. You can just put everything in Joseph's lap."

The wise men stayed seated, playing with baby Jesus, who was beginning to stir and look up at the proceedings with sleepy interest. The narrator began the end of the story, and the angel choir scooted close to the side of the manger scene for one final song.

"Now," said the narrator, "All this was done that it might be fulfilled which was spoken of the Lord by the prophet saying, Behold, a virgin shall be with child and shall bring forth a son, and they shall call his name Emmanuel, which being interpreted is, God with us. And He is. The prophecy has been fulfilled. The light of the world has come! Ladies and gentlemen, stand and help us celebrate his birth today."

The classical background music came to a sudden halt and refused to cooperate further. I ran to the keyboard and began playing to prevent any further dead air.

The angel choir crowded in close behind Mary and Joseph as they stood up. The wise men and shepherds shoved together, until a tight little huddle stood around the makeshift nativity, looking down at the baby. Jesus closed his eyes again. He lay in the straw, long eyelashes draped against his cheeks, one arm flung over the side of the manger, as he nodded off again into oblivion.

Shane faced the actors in his flowing white robe, raised his arms, and took a deep breath, and they were off. Waving his arms with all of his might, an enthusiastic pastor/Angel Gabriel/choir director, led the fidgeting cast in an off-key version of "Oh Come Let Us Adore

Him". He turned around to face the audience.

"Let's all just sing that together one more time," Shane said.

One by one, voices from the audience joined in the refrain,

Oh come let us adore Him
Oh come let us adore Him
Oh come let us adore Him
Christ the Lord

For He alone is worthy
For He alone is worthy
For He alone is worthy
Christ the Lord

The room slowly filled with the sound of voices lifted high. As the anthem gained momentum, I looked around at our multicultural church, singing together, celebrating the advent of the One who quietly entered the world on that lonely night so long ago.

Then the voices slowly died down, the song faded, the fidgeting stopped, and a profound stillness rested upon each one of us. No one wanted to move in that quiet moment.

Christmas was here.

THE NIGHT EVERYTHING CHANGED

It was the biggest wedding that we could put together on a small budget, and it was a blur.

I was tired. I forgot to put flowers in the flower girl's basket, so she walked down the aisle scattering fresh green leaves instead. The platform was full of wedding attendants behind us. Eight guys stood in penguin suits and eight girls wore jewel-toned satin empire dresses covered in sheer organza. During the eternity-long ceremony, my miniature bride nodded off and slowly collapsed downward into a soft little heap of sleeping satin.

My nose itched from perfume and pollen in the air. I stood across from him as a skinny, young girl in a white tulle ball gown. My long, gauzy veil was handcrafted by my mother, and the headband was a fairy tale of tiny white flowers and grapevine sprigs. There was a hazy crowd of guests to my right. My vocal coach began to sing.

As her voice soared into the rafters, I realized that we had not practiced the ring ceremony. My mind began to race, trying to decide when would be a good time for him to slip it on my hand before we were pronounced man and wife.

When we had picked out wedding rings several months before, the salesman asked, "And what would the gentleman like to wear?"

Shane's response was, "I don't want one. I wouldn't know which finger to wear it on."

"Well," the salesman answered, "You could always wear it on a chain around your neck."

Shane turned to me and started laughing.

"Could you see me out somewhere preaching with my shirt halfway unbuttoned like I've come from the 70's, with my chest hair hanging out and my wedding ring dangling from a thick gold chain? That's okay. I'll be fine without it."

The salesman was disappointed that he would not have another sale, but he was pleased with the commission he would make from the diamond-encrusted band that we chose to wrap around with my engagement ring. It was lovely and looked like a line of sparkling fire and I was ecstatic.

But now here we were in the middle of our wedding, and we had forgotten about doing any sort of ring ceremony.

As the song went on, I hissed at Shane out of the side of my mouth, "The ring! What are we going to do? When are you going to put it on me?"

Shane's eyes flew open wide. He whispered, "Oh no. I'm sorry."

I thought for a minute.

"Okay, here's what we can do," I said, "In about twenty seconds I can turn around and smile at my bridesmaids while the song is still going. You pull the ring out of your pocket, and when I turn back around, just hold it out toward me and I will act surprised. Then you can just slip it on my hand before the song is over and we'll stand there and look down at my hand and ooh and ahh for a minute."

And that is what we did. The final strains of "All I Ask of You" faded away as a diamond wedding band slid over my fourth finger and he held my hand in his and smiled up at me.

I had my own surprise waiting. I picked up the microphone and looked down into his eyes and began to sing, "You are so beautiful to me."

I heard sniffles begin all around me. Tears welled up in his eyes and began to slide down his cheeks. He mopped them away repeatedly with a handkerchief, and I was transported back in time to the night we met four years before, when he ran past me and I fell in love.

I was on vacation in Texas, and I was seventeen. He was one of the central actors in a play, and it was the first time I had ever seen him. The lights in the auditorium were turned down low when he dashed down the center aisle. I burst into silent tears and was thankful for the darkness that hid my sudden emotions. I found myself silently whispering, "*I love him. Oh my God. I love him.*" And that was the night everything changed. His name was Shane.

He had to be a good eight inches shorter than me. His hair was brown. He ran with a distinct hobble. I learned later that it was because his ankles were fused together from multiple surgeries and did not bend. There was something unusual about his arms and hands. His arms were short. Some of his fingers were missing. And he was perfect.

I made up my mind to meet him as soon as the event was over, regardless of how it had to happen. He sat up on stage, and I waited at the front. He stepped down the stairs and began to walk toward the back of the auditorium. I followed him and my heart hammered in my throat and I called his name. He did not look back. I walked out into the hallway behind him, and still he barged ahead like a freight train. I decided that my pursuit was making me look shameless, so I found his sister and asked her to introduce us.

I wore a short black suit with very high heels. I stood in the hall and adjusted my hair and felt self-conscious. I was glad that my hair was curly that night. I heard his sister's voice somewhere near my shoulder.

"Randa, I want you to meet my brother, Shane."

With my heels on, I towered a good ten inches above him. He looked up at me and I felt myself falling far down into his eyes, oceans of brilliant blue.

"Hello," I said, "I'm Randa."

He smiled politely and shook my hand, and I stopped breathing. *Get a grip, Randa,* I told myself, *He's just saying hello.*

"It's good to meet you," he said. I smiled and tried to tell him, *I love you,* with my eyes. But he turned around and walked away.

I felt a sad disappointment come over me. I had just blatantly chased down the man of my dreams, and he was walking away from me. *Oh well,* I said to myself, *at least you tried.* I leaned against the wall for a moment and swallowed and tried to smile. The hall was crowded with people, and I began pushing my way back through the crowd to find my friends. I felt a tap on my arm and glanced over. He was there, and he was smiling.

"We're going to Chili's," he said, "Would you like to go with me to get something to eat?"

I did not hesitate. "Yes."

It would not be a date with just the two of us staring into each other's eyes as I thought it would be. There were several in our party, but I did not care. This was destiny and we had just grabbed it by the horns.

At the restaurant voices roared around us. He leaned in close and whispered that he had walked away from me because he thought I was much older than he was. After he found out that we were the same age, he canceled a date with another girl who he was supposed to take out that night.

"You see," he explained, "She didn't really want to go out with me, and I was just going along with it to get my dad off my back."

"Well," I said, "That worked out pretty great. I actually want to be with you, and I'm glad you decided to stand her up."

The girl was also at the restaurant, and I heard an ornery little demon whispering in my ear. "Shane, I'll be right back," I said. I walked over to the table where she sat with her friends and stuck out my hand.

"Hi, I'm Randa. I just wanted to meet the girl that Shane was supposed to go out with tonight."

She shook my hand without a word and I turned around and came back to the table. A continual stream of people floated by our table to say hello and give Shane the thumbs-up. The quiet boy was popular. We grinned at each other and ordered our food.

I heard an occasional quiet comment from him, and our hands not-so-accidentally brushed several times, and my heart raced. I had had boyfriends before, but this was new. It was different, and I knew in the depths of my heart that I was stuck for life. I pulled out my camera and handed it to his friend.

"Here, will you take a picture of us on our first date?"

From the corner of my eye, I could see Shane start to smile.

"How do you want to pose for the picture of our First Date?" he said.

"Hmmm," I said, 'How about if we just look at each other?"

So we turned and looked into each other's eyes and smiled, and that was when lightning sizzled around us and we slid into each other's souls. Time stopped for me.

"Whoa," his friend said, "Did you feel that?"

I felt my face turning deep red. The lump in my throat was so thick that I could not talk, so I just nodded and looked down at the table.

When it was time to leave, I stood up and banged my head against the galvanized steel bucket that served as a pendant lampshade above our table. We went outside and sat in the car and looked at each other in silence. He reached over and took my hand in his, and it took my breath away. I felt my heart constrict inside of my chest and knew I had to come up with some sort of plan so that I could see him again before my family headed back to Michigan. I did not care that I was staying a hundred miles away from San Antonio. We would just have to figure out a way to get back here.

I slipped my hand into my purse and found my glasses. I began to chatter to distract him from my real purpose. I waved my hands around, and finally gave my glasses a casual sling behind me. They landed in the backseat of his father's car. Now I would have to return to San Antonio to retrieve them.

That night as I rode back with my family to my grandmother's ranch, I sat in the back seat of the car. The rest of my family grinned and nudged each other and waggled their eyebrows at me, trying to tease me, but I could not talk. I breathed a deep sigh and rested my head against the window.

I stared up into the hill country night sky. It was perfectly clear. I could see the constellations and the singing stars and the whiteness of the Milky Way. The moon was a brilliant white and the hills and scrub trees stood out in stark silhouettes around us. I heard the muted slap of the tires as they thumped over the yellow reflector lights in the road and I stared out into the deep pools of shadow that surrounded our car as we flew through the night.

My life had just changed without notice, but I knew that I was in the hands of One who cared about the smallest things in my life. I felt a deep, unfamiliar peace settle over me. My frantic soul began to feel a rest that I had never encountered before. It was quieting.

Four years later, after many ups and downs, we stood pledging our vows before six hundred people. We were hitched for good. We ran out of the reception and someone dumped an entire bag of rice down my clothes. As we raced away in his red Mustang and turned out onto the road, I heard an unsolicited little voice inside my head whispering, *"What have you done? You can't go back now."*

So I turned off that fear-inducing voice and turned to the man I loved. And I have been turning to him ever since.

The wedding bouquet has faded on a shelf. The gown that was stepped on and torn by someone during our reception remains unrepaired. At times the romance has turned wildly unromantic.

We have been through fire together, but it has made us vastly stronger and served to draw us closer. Roses are charming, and I will never turn up my nose at a bottle of expensive perfume, but fifteen years and three children later, I have learned that the most precious pieces of this romance are the unexpected, small things.

When we hear the same thing that strikes our funny bones, and we bite our cheeks and our eyes meet across the room and dance with silent shared convulsions of laughter. When he rubs my back because he knows I have spent a grinding day at work. When I alter his long-sleeve shirts by hand so that he has normal-looking dress shirts, and I catch my breath thinking about how handsome he looks in them. When we are penniless and still find a way to spend quality time together. When we stay awake on a week night until 2:00 a.m., talking and commiserating and sharing dreams and heartbreak, and realize that we will be good for nothing the next morning.

That is when I realize for the thousandth time how blessed I am to get to walk by the side of my best friend on this journey of life, for richer and poorer, in sickness and in health, to love, honor and cherish, until death parts us.

Please God, let the adventure continue until we grow so old that the shapes of each other's smiles are all we know. Help me to always treasure this lovely man as I should, this steadfast one whom I have taken for granted at times. This companion that you wrote into the pages of my life before I ever read them. This blessing. This immeasurable blessing.

UNCERTAIN IDENTITY

It was my fourth consecutive night of severe insomnia.

Sleeping aids were out of the question. They always knocked me out for several days, and I was good for nothing afterward. I figured the dead of night was as good of a time as any to converse with my Creator, so I decided to try talking to God until I was too tired to keep my eyes open. Sometimes that worked pretty quickly, and sometimes it did not work until 4 a.m.

This was one of those insomniac nights, and I finally fell asleep around 3:30 a.m. I was already several levels down in the deep, hard netherworld of slumber. I was having dreams that were utter madness. Devon herself awakened after a frightening dream, and tiptoed into my bedroom, trying to find comfort.

Why she decided to stand next to my bed and stare me awake, rather than attempting to shake me or say my name, I will never know. But it worked.

I woke up just slightly and opened my eyes. In my severe state of grogginess, all I saw was a blurry, silent figure standing right next to my bed, staring down at me in the dark. My bleary eyes did not recognize her. Instead, I was convinced that this was a demonic apparition sent from Hell to attack our family.

I felt a sudden adrenaline surge that made my feet tingle. My heart constricted and began to clench like it does when I look down from a very high building. I felt like I could not breathe, but I knew that I had to do something to make this "thing" get away from me.

Having been startled straight out of a dead sleep, I was also having trouble speaking clearly. My tongue felt several inches thick. I sat up and pointed my finger in her face and sputtered what I thought was a clear and distinct sentence. What I intended to say was, "In the name of Jesus."

What actually came out of my mouth was a low-pitched, "Jeeeethuth. Jethuth. Jethuuuuth."

It sounded like a mix between a dying grunt and an unworldly moan. And that is all that would come out of my mouth at that moment. I struggled to gain control of my language skills. My poor child. She reached out and tapped me on the shoulder.

"Mom? Mom?" she said. There was a distinct quaver in her voice.

But I was vehement.

"In the NAME of Jeeethuth," I said, "Youuuu!" I threw my pointer finger toward her again. "Youuu ginn AWAY from me and leeeave thith houth!"

I was still wrapped in a cobweb of sleep, and there was no convincing me that this was my daughter standing next to me. Devon tried to awaken me four times more, with the same type of inebriated rebuke from me, before she finally became completely petrified. Her loud wail of terror pierced through my sleep-induced fog.

"Mooooom! Mooom!" she sobbed and leaned over me. "Wake up! It's just me. It's Devon!"

I opened my eyes completely and recognized my daughter for the first time. She stared at me with a wild-eyed expression that indicated she would dart away from me if I even moved a muscle in her direction. I slowly realized my sleepy mistake. I covered my mouth and looked up at her.

"Oh, baby. I am SO sorry," I said, "Devon, I was dead asleep. I didn't know it was you standing there, and I thought... I thought... Oh dear."

I looked down, horrified at the fear I had just caused my firstborn child, and I felt my composure melt.

"It's okay, Mom," she whimpered, "You just scared me really bad like you did that time when – when you inhaled some helium out of a balloon as a joke. Remember how it changed your voice? And then you called my name? You said, 'Hey, Devon. What's up?' And then I started screaming and crying and jumping up and down because I didn't know what was wrong with you and I thought maybe you had gone crazy."

Her words came out in a rush and she buried her head in my shoulder. We began to heehaw in uncontrollable whinnying laugher in the pitch dark room as I held her close, and the bed shook.

I worried that she might be traumatized from her experience. But several nights later at dinner, she pointed across the table at me and said, "Jeeeesus! Jesus!" in a perfect imitation of my late-night exorcism performance.

She threw her head back and let out a wide-open mouth laugh from the core of her being, and as my cheeks turned red, I knew she was going to be okay – and that I would never live that one down.

AMAZING GRACE

I watched from the porch that afternoon as the cousins consulted nose-to-nose in the yard, one blonde boy and one skinny girl with light brown hair. Their eyeglass frames were almost touching. Grace put her hand on her hip as she gestured to Gage and gave in-depth instructions for the scene they were to act out in their game of pretend. He nodded seriously, bowed to her, and then assumed a pose with his knee to the ground as if he were about to run a race. Grace glided away from him with her hands clasped behind her back, and then gave him a furtive glance over her shoulder. Gage's eyebrows stood high on his forehead as he waited in happy anticipation for her next command.

She raised both of her arms out to the side and stood on one leg like a stork. She slowly wobbled from side to side for several seconds, attempting to find her balance. She wrinkled her brow and assumed a terrified expression, then threw her head back toward the sky shouting, "Come quickly, Gage! Help me! I see a tiger chasing my flock of dolphins through the forest!"

Gage sprang up from his crouching position and ran toward her with a gallant fist in the air, yelling, "I will help you! I will save your dolphins!"

Clouds of dust kicked up behind their bare feet as they dashed around the corner of the house toward the backyard. My shoulders were shaking with laughter as I stood up and headed back inside to share their latest adventure with my sister, Keli.

I began to remember the day that Grace was born in that chilly December eight years before. She was 73 days early when she came into the world.

Keli had gone in for her second ultrasound. Her blood pressure was high and her doctor was concerned. She sat on the exam table, feeling like a giant blueberry. Her stomach bulged under her blue sundress and turquoise t-shirt. Blue flip-flops encased her swollen toes. The doctor gazed at the ultrasound machine, muttering to herself and spouting medical terminology that made no sense. Confused and frustrated, Keli asked her to please explain herself.

The doctor replied without looking up. "What I mean," she said, "Is that you are going to have a baby today. She has not grown in five weeks and your blood pressure is too high. I am going to write the orders for you to be admitted."

"Excuse me," Keli said.

She lifted herself off of the exam table and waddled out of the room with a blank expression. She had gone to the doctor's office for what she thought was a routine sonogram. Keli hid in the restroom and panicked as she sobbed into a wad of paper towels. She had specifically prayed for a girl with a spitfire spirit, and now she was faced with the sudden realization that her girl was going to be born in just a few short hours.

Her husband, Justin, was working deep in the country and unable to be contacted, as his phone was out of range. Keli had nothing packed for a hospital stay, and was completely unprepared for the arrival of a baby. The room in their house that was to be the baby's nursery was still piled with boxes and personal belongings. There were no diapers, baby care items or any kind of furniture. No baby shower had taken place. It was still too early. She only had two little zip-up sleepers.

Keli called me and informed me that the

baby was coming. I jumped up and ran out of my office to head toward the hospital in Austin, 80 miles away. I prayed aloud as I drove. I realized that Keli had no baby clothes or blankets, so I stopped at a store on the way. In my state of confusion, I did not think about the fact that the baby would be too small to even wear preemie clothing, much less newborn size. When I arrived at the hospital two hours later with my arms full of baby clothes, I realized that they were much too large and I felt foolish. I dumped them in a large shopping bag, where they waited for months until Grace was big enough to wear them.

Meanwhile, my mother held Keli's hand in the delivery room as an emergency C-section was performed. Keli heard the doctor say, "Look at this!" and then my mother glimpsed a tiny, gray human in the air, being held upside down by her feet. As the baby was carried away to be cleaned up and weighed, her arms and legs dangled and her miniature head lolled between the nurse's index and middle fingers. From shoulders to bottom, her entire trunk fit into the nurse's hand. She was 16 inches long and weighed a total of 2 pounds 10 ounces.

Keli turned to my mother and whispered, "Is she okay?" and then she heard the smack that was applied to the baby's bottom and the resultant angry wail. The doctor came around to stand next to her.

"Your baby survived because of your high blood pressure," she told Keli. "The umbilical cord was wrapped around her neck and was tied in a double knot. That is why she was not growing. Your high blood pressure still managed to force blood and nutrients through the cord, though, and that is what kept her alive."

Before Grace was whisked away to the neonatal intensive care unit, she was wrapped into a tiny bundle and held up to Keli for inspection. Her face was the circumference of a nasal aspirator bulb. She was eerily pale and silent, and her eyes were closed.

Keli began to cry and asked the nurse, "Is she dead?"

"Oh, no, no. She's just asleep," the nurse said, trying to comfort her. Keli closed her eyes and nodded off to sleep.

Justin arrived at the hospital and rushed to Labor and Delivery. As he entered the hallway, he looked up in time to see his tiny newborn daughter being wheeled past him to ICU. He felt pure happiness as he realized that he was now a father to the little scrap of humanity that he only saw for a brief second before she was taken down the hall.

In ICU, the medical team began to hook

up Grace to IVs and give her shots to build her lung capacity. She was placed into an incubator with holes in the sides to allow her to be cared for without the top of the incubator having to be opened.

When visitors were allowed, I came in and stood next to the incubator, looking down at her. She was so thin. She had minimal fat on her body, and she was covered in saran wrap to help her to retain heat. I could see pathways of veins showing through translucent skin that was too fragile to be stroked. Tubes ran out of her nose and mouth, and various IVs were attached to the top of her head, arms and wrists.

Multiple heart monitor tabs were stuck to her chest. The identification bracelet covered the bottom half of her forearm. The lids of her eyes were dark purple and bruised, and she looked like she had two identical shiners. She lay in the incubator with her eyes shut, breathing in and out with the assistance of oxygen. She was fighting to survive. I felt helpless.

I went back to Keli's room and told her that she had a beautiful baby girl who was doing just fine. I kissed her forehead, and walked out of the hospital holding back tears. I made it to the dark parking garage and climbed into my car before I broke down into uncontrollable sobs. Shivering with cold, I leaned over my steering wheel, weeping and praying with all of my heart that God would allow our little one to survive.

Keli was unable to see her baby for several days. She lay in her hospital bed and cried as she recovered and waited to hold Grace. Justin came to NICU and stared at Grace for hours on end, willing her to live. "I love you, baby," he said. Every time Grace heard his voice, her face crinkled into a smile and she began to wriggle her arms and legs.

On the fifth day, Keli was taken to NICU and scrubbed down so that she could talk to her daughter for the first time. She leaned forward in her rocking chair and rested her head against the incubator, speaking in a high, soft voice. "Hey, beautiful. It's Mamma. I love you," she said over and over. She reached through the incubator wall and placed her finger on Grace's arm. "I love you so much, Gracie."

After ten days, Keli was finally allowed to hold Grace. The baby was lifted out of the incubator, attached to all of her tubes. Her diaper was the size of a Post-It note. Her knees were drawn up to her chest and her toes splayed outward. Keli reached upward and Grace was carefully placed into her two hands. Keli tilted her head down as she pulled her baby close to cuddle underneath her chin. Grace was no bigger than a child's football when she rolled up into a comfortable position. Keli's hand covered her completely. The tips of Keli's fingers rested against the top of the baby's head and Grace relaxed against Keli's collarbone with a whispering sigh. A softness stole over Keli's face as she began to rock back and forth with her baby cupped in her hands.

Grace finally went home at the age of 5 weeks, weighing a whopping 4 pounds, 8 ounces. She was too small for her car seat, so extra layers of blankets were packed around her for support. When she arrived at my mother's house to be changed and fed, the entire worried family, grandparents, aunts, uncles and cousins, all crowded into the bedroom to make sure she had survived the trip in one piece.

Six months later it was June, and she finally fit into the newborn-sized clothing that I had shoved into a bag the day she arrived. She was the perfect size for cuddling. Later that month, Keli was driving their white minivan down a two-lane highway in Granite Shoals. The lake next to the road reflected the bright morning sun, and Grace was secured in her car seat. Traffic was backed up on the hill in the oncoming lane. A young man in line became impatient and decided to drive into the oncoming lane to pass the cars in front of him. As Keli came over the hill going 55 miles per hour, there was no time for her to try to evade or brake.

The two vehicles crashed into each other

head-on at full speed, and then everything went into slow motion for Keli. One second she was driving to give someone a haircut, and the next she was flying through the air seeing a thousand stars roaring towards her. She wondered momentarily if she was dead.

There was a giant boom as several tons of metal slammed against each other. Rubber shrieked against the pavement as the vehicles spun and finally came to a stop. The smell of oil and dust and smoke filled the van. Keli's safety belt bit deep into her chest, bruising her severely. It restricted her from breathing properly or being able to move.

Silence filled the air for several seconds and then people came running to help. Keli could not move. Her left leg was broken at the thigh and her right foot was embedded in the accelerator pedal.

No one knew that a baby was even involved in the accident for several moments. The force of the impact was so violent that Grace's car seat was torn from the bars that secured the seat to its base. Still strapped into her car seat, Grace was thrown into the air and landed face-down in the back of the minivan, where she remained hidden until Keli regained consciousness and began to whisper to the police officer who was working to extricate her from the vehicle.

"My baby. Where is my baby?" she croaked.

The emergency responders located and removed Grace from the back of the minivan, but were unaware that her left thigh was also broken. Grace whimpered several times but never cried out loud. Her injuries remained undiscovered until she was x-rayed at the hospital.

Keli and the driver of the other vehicle were life-flighted together to the hospital, and Grace was taken by ambulance.

When I arrived at the emergency room, Keli lay on an exam table moaning in pain. Her long hair hung down from the table and brushed against the floor as my mother picked glass out of her scalp. The room was stark white and freezing cold. I was in my first trimester of pregnancy and felt a giant wave of nausea wash over me at the sight of the x-rays of Keli's broken legs being held up and examined by the doctor. I fought off dizziness and sat down on a rolling exam chair, but the whir and click of machines and beeping monitors and painful weeping all combined into a cacophony of sound that overwhelmed me. I did not know what to say or do. I escaped and went to find Grace.

She lay in a separate room in her newborn onesie, waiting to be examined. Her skin was clammy and her short hair was flattened against her head, except for one small curl that stood up on top of her skull and refused to lie down. Her thin legs were sprawled. No one knew yet that one was broken. She looked up at me and a small whine escaped her. I put my hand next to her cheek and began to speak to her in a low voice, hoping to soothe her.

"It's okay, baby. You're gonna be fine, sweetheart. It's okay."

She was hungry. She licked her lips and sucked on her fist, but her mother was in surgery and unable to nurse her. I assembled a bottle of formula and Grace took a few swallows. Her eyes slowly closed in weary slumber. She was still in shock, and twitched and hiccupped in her sleep.

I spent the rest of the day taking turns with my parents watching Keli and Grace.

Grace was put into a body cast to prevent her from trying to crawl. It encased both legs and came up to cover her waist and lower back. A wooden dowel was inserted into the bottom of the casts, stretching across from one ankle to another to provide some stability when she needed to be picked up and held. There was a small area in the cast to pull out soiled diapers

and wriggle a fresh one into place with the help
of a shoehorn.

Rods were inserted into Keli's leg, but she
did not receive a cast. The very next morning
following her surgery, a physical therapist came
into the room and made her begin walking with
the aid of a walker and several strong medical
assistants. She made the excruciating trips down
the hall and back, and I heard her screams of
pain as she began the task of recovery.

She was heavily medicated, and shared
with me the hallucinations that were her drugged
reality. Several times I hid my grin as she told
me about the red dragon that she saw sitting in
the hospital room in the early morning while I
was asleep in the chair next to her bed. And she
was convinced that my sister, Krystal, and I were
mistreating her. Thinking we could not hear her
from two feet away, she put up her hand in front
of her mouth as if to tell the nurse a secret, and
then in a loud voice told her how mean her
sisters were being, and could the hospital staff
please do something to stop us.

When Keli was finally able to walk with
the walker several days later, she and Grace were
released from the hospital. They stayed at my
parents' home for three months until Keli was
able to walk again on her own. The process of
healing was a vicious, heartbreaking season, but
they survived. Today, Keli has scars on both

legs, but she is able to walk perfectly. And Grace runs like the wind.

At the age of 8, Grace has now grown into a tall, slim soul who is both wise and unintentionally hilarious. She is a tough little fighter who is intensely protective of those she loves.

I knew of her passion for shielding her mother from hurt, but it became very evident to me one day when Grace was 3 years old. She sat across from me at the dinner table with Keli. As a joke, I mouthed, "Watch this," to a friend who sat with me.

I reached over and poked Keli on the arm. Grace's dark hazel eyes slid toward me and purple shadows began to appear around them. She gave me a hard stare with her chin jutted out. I had been warned. I started to smile.

"Watch out," Keli said, "She won't let you get much further."

"Okay," I said.

I poked Keli again. "Keli!" I said in a loud voice, "I am tired of you acting like this! You had better stop it!"

Grace's face flushed and she began to growl. I looked over at her. Her eyes glittered with unshed tears of rage. I realized that my joke had gone too far and I started to apologize.

"Baby, I am very sorry. I'm really not mad at your mamma. I was just playing."

I reached across the table toward her and she snapped her arm back away from me. She growled again and glared at me with her eyebrows drawn together. She threw her index finger in my face and looked me in the eyes. In a low voice that was full of anger, she bit off her words.

"I. will. track. you. down."

That was the last time I ever pretended to antagonize anyone in front of her.

Grace's resilient exterior is far stronger than many teenage boys, but she carries a tender, sensitive heart. She is wildly unique and loves to dress herself in mismatched clothing. On any given day you might see her with her hair in various ponytails, wearing red striped legwarmers over paisley leggings with a pink floral shirt and mint green skirt.

Her nose is constantly in a book. When it comes to identifying bugs and other creatures, she is a walking encyclopedia. She will spend twenty minutes explaining how to catch, care for and dispose of lizard, spiders and stray deer.

She walked into the kitchen the other day and informed her mother that she was about to perform an ancient Chinese dance that she had just made up a few moments before. Then she proceeded to execute a series of measured stomps, solemn claps, several whistles and a wild jump and twist at the end that resembled an Irish jig.

When she brushes her unruly hair out of her face and opens her mouth, a shrewd statement usually issues forth mixed with oblivious hilarity which causes the adults in the room to quickly avert their faces, lest she see the laughter she has created and be crushed.

Riding in the truck the other day, she proclaimed in a matter-of-fact tone that she hated rock stars. When asked why, she stated, "Because they worship rocks."

The world never sparkled so bright before as it has since Grace has come into it. She is quaint and unexpected. She loves violently and is riotous in her celebration of life. She was the miracle our family prayed would survive, and then she became the shocking blessing who later we realized we needed even more than she needed us.

She is the amazing Grace.

THE FORMALDEHYDE BABY

(Thalidomide is a drug that was prescribed in the mid-1950's to pregnant women for morning sickness. After being linked to thousands of multiple birth defects and infant mortality around the world, including severely deformed and/or shortened arms and legs, and sometimes a complete lack of limbs, thalidomide was withdrawn from the market in the 1960's.)

"Do you have life insurance? Would your family be taken care of if – God forbid – you were to die tomorrow?"

The salesman's eyes danced with the prospect of another commission and he waited patiently for us to bite. So we did. We were the naïve young parents with our first child, traveling through the hills of Tennessee. We nodded and looked at each other with alarm. Our 14-month-old Devon would be starting college in just eighteen short years.

We agreed that those years would flash before our eyes. Two hours later, we walked out, armed with a college fund, universal life insurance, term life insurance, and every other investment vehicle that he was able to convince us to purchase.

"Now, don't forget that a nurse will come by to do your blood draws next week!" he called out as we were leaving. We nodded and kept walking, ready to escape.

The appointed day rolled around and the mobile blood draw representative knocked on the door. I opened it and looked up, up, up until my gaze reached her wide forehead. It floated up in the sky several feet above. Her name was Janelle.

She was an Amazon with wild brown hair that frizzed out from her head in crazy disarray with a white nurse's cap perched on top. Her shoulders filled the doorway. She yanked at the hem of her button-down white uniform. It fit her like a sausage casing about to burst. She wore sensible rubber-soled white shoes with thick support hose. She looked the part of a no-nonsense medical provider. She was strong. I half expected her to pull out a pair of forceps to grasp my skull and swing me around the room until she became bored and sent me flying into a wall.

She looked at both of us and became interested when she saw Shane. She stared at his hands and arms without comment for a full minute before turning back to me.

"Okay, let's just get started with you, ma'am, and then we'll take care of your husband. Now, how about we sit out here at this table and we'll answer a few questions."

We sat and waited as she pulled up her cat-eye reading glasses that hung from a chain around her neck. She adjusted them at the end of her nose and then hunched over the table and thumbed through our paperwork. She breathed heavily through her mouth. She obviously had some sort of allergy that blocked her nasal passages.

"Uh-huh. Yep. Yep. Looks real good. Uh-huh."

She glanced over at Shane from time to time and then returned to her review of our records. She stopped thumbing and cocked an eyebrow at me.

"Now, ma'am, how much would you say you weighed overall?"

"How about if I just write that down for you?" I said. "Shane has never known how much I weigh and he's not going to find out now."

"Sure, honey, that'll be fine," she said, "Just give it to me and I'll read it."

I scribbled on a slip of paper, folded it and handed it to her. She looked down and examined it with her lip poked out. She nodded and then began to fill in her form as she slowly repeated my weight aloud with enough volume to be heard in the next county.

"Yer a big healthy girl, alright," she concluded.

My face turned purple and Shane snickered.

I elbowed him. "Oh, just you wait. You're next."

"Alright, honey," she said, "Just roll up your sleeve. That's it. I'm gonna pop this here little band around your arm to get the blood pressure goin', and then we'll give you a little stick. It's really not all that bad."

The circulation in my arm was suddenly cut off as she twisted and pulled a stretchy rubber strip tight around my arm. My fingertips began to tingle.

"Go on," she said, "Flex that arm for me, baby."

She tapped the inside of my arm searching for a good vein and then thwacked at the vein with a flick of her middle finger. She was blissfully unaware of her strength. A welt began to rise on the surface of my skin. She jabbed in a needle that appeared to me to be about three feet long, and I felt a stinging sensation like a bumblebee had just flown into my bloodstream.

"Good. Yer doing real good. Just a few more minutes." She hummed and puttered around as my life blood was sucked out of my arm, and then she yanked out the needle. She slapped a cotton ball on the puncture wound and taped it down.

"All good to go, ma'am. Now let's take care of that husband of yours."

She reached out and took Shane's right arm in her meaty hand. She wound up to begin her tap-thwack-flick routine on his inner elbow and then stopped short with a look of confusion.

"Now - huh... You don't rightly have no - I mean - well," she turned to me, "His arms ain't bendin' and there ain't a soft spot where I can find a vein."

"That's right," I said. There was no need to reiterate the obvious.

She glared at him as if she expected him to grow a new arm right then and there. Shane patiently waited to be stabbed with the needle. Janelle stood there stroking her chin and talking to herself as she examined him from head to toe.

"How 'bout that other arm?" she finally said, "Let's try your left arm."

She twisted and screwed his arm around in windmills trying to find a good vein, but none was to be found. She held up a finger as an idea hit her.

"I recollect a time I did a draw from a person's ankle. Let's see if that'll work."

Shane rolled up his pant leg and Janelle poked around with her finger and then a needle. No such luck. She was becoming desperate and agitated, upset that she was unable to perform her assigned job.

"Lemme see. Now, if you two can hang on for a couple of minutes, I'm gonna step around the corner and make a call to my office. We normally have to draw quite a bit of blood, but I'm gonna try to get them to make an exception for you and just let me do a finger stick."

So we settled down in our chairs. She stepped outside the door and left it open, giving us ample opportunity to listen in on her conversation.

"Hey, Marge? Yeah, this is Janelle." Her voice boomed with unusual strength.

"Listen. I – I got me an unusual situation goin' on here... I need to get permission to do a finger stick instead of a normal draw. I cain't find a vein... No, it ain't that... He's missin' most of his fingers and his arms don't bend, and I just cain't find a vein... That's right."

She lowered her voice several decibels, but we could still her as loud as if she were standing next to us.

"What we've got here," she murmured in a gravelly undertone, "Is one of them formaldehyde babies... Yep. Just like they had back in the sixties with all them deformities."

Back at the table my mouth fell open and my head swung around toward Shane. Surely I had not heard her correctly. But he was staring at me with uncontrollable laughter in his eyes.

Simultaneously we hissed at each other, "For-MAL-dehyde babies?!?"

We considered her statement for several shocked seconds and then collapsed forward on the table in helpless, silent laughter. Every time I calmed down and began to gain control, Shane would begin to shake all over with giggles. The cycle continued for several minutes until Janelle returned.

She was all business. "Well, they said I could try a finger stick. Let's go ahead and try that."

Janelle performed a finger stick as Shane continued to cackle. I leaned on the table, trembling and holding my head in my hands, still snorting like a horse with a cold.

Janelle watched both of us out of the corner of her eye with genuine concern. She was puzzled at our reaction over a simple blood test. She scraped a bit of Shane's blood onto a slide, threw it into a baggy, and then hoofed it out of there.

The door closed behind Janelle and we lost all composure. She surely must have thought we were slightly insane. Yells of hilarity bounced off the walls and echoed through the room as I pounded the table with my fists. My stomach began to ache from laughing so hard.

"Aaaagh! Hahaha!" I howled. "She really

did it. She called you – she called you – " I could not finish my sentence because I was overcome once again with a spasm that caused my eyes to close.

Shane had removed his glasses to wipe his streaming eyes and then laid his head on the table, shaking silently. He sat back up at my comment.

"I know! Hee hee hee!" he shouted, "She – hee – heeee – hee! And she called you FAT! Oh! Oh! I can't take it anymore!" He leaned back in his chair, shaking and kicking his feet back and forth.

It took us a good fifteen minutes to return to earth. I looked up and saw Devon standing in front of us with her hands on her hips. She was becoming worried as she stood watching us. Our poise was gone and there would be no getting it back that day, but it was time to calm down.

"Come on, baby," I said, taking her hand, "Let's go put your coat on and get some ice cream."

And so we did.

THANKFUL

"Okay, okay, I've got one! Who were the preachers who broke out of a Roman jail at midnight?" Shane asks.

"Oooh! I know! Paul and Psoriasis!" Gage yells.

It is Tuesday night and we are eating pizza and playing Bible trivia again.

"This one's for Devon," Shane says, "What did Samson use to kill a thousand Philistines?"

"Um..." she stares down at the table, trying to remember.

Shane prompts her. "The jawbone of a...."

Devon's eyebrows shoot up in excitement.

"The jawbone of a TURTLE!" she yells, pointing straight at Shane.

"A donkey! It was a donkey!" Gage says. Devon's countenance darkens and she scowls at her brother.

"Good try, baby," Shane says. "Now a question for Benjamin."

Benjamin grins from his high chair. "Me question."

"What color is Mamma's shirt, Benjamin?"

"BLUE!" Benjamin crows, proud to have the correct answer. Claps and cheers erupt from his brother and sister.

I watch the children laughing around the table with Shane. They adore their father. He wrestles with them on the floor like a big bear. Several pairs of their glasses have been broken this way, but the memories they have when they look back will have been worth that extra cost.

They notice everything about him and they try to mimic him. When he awakens in the morning, his legs are stiff and his ankles hurt, and he has to hobble around for the first few minutes to warm up his joints. The other morning, Benjamin and Gage came into the bedroom as Shane was getting out of bed. They followed their father across the room and into the bathroom like two little wobbly penguins, taking halting steps and flapping their arms. Gage beamed up at me and said, "Mamma, look! I can walk just like Daddy!"

At ten years of age, Devon has already grown taller than her father, a fact that makes her very proud. She backs up to him and says, "Stand up straight, Daddy."

She adjusts his shoulders against her back and then measures the difference in their height with her hand.

"I'm 5 feet tall! I have you beat by one inch!" she says, "Mom, look!"

And then she rests her head on his shoulder and they slow dance together through the living room and the look of happy wonder on Shane's face is almost too much to watch.

* * * * *

I sit next to the window one late Sunday afternoon immersed in a book. The atmosphere is clammy and damp and beginning to drizzle. The light outside is dim and casts a grayish-green hue over the entire backyard. The oak tree branches bend low over the ground. The grass is knee-high and brilliant green. Patches of white rain lilies bloom in the far corner next to the fence.

A tiny four-year-old body topped with a curly head flashes past me and hurtles through the open back door. I come back to earth and realize that Gage has run out into the yard without a stitch of clothing. I put down my book and prepare to yell at him to get back inside, when I notice what he is doing.

His pale white back and bony shoulder blades present themselves to me as he kneels over the tall grass, pulling up a handful of rain lilies by the roots with care, and then he tops off the little bundle with a dirty twig. He marches back inside the house with an expectant smile, clutching his bouquet high above his head. I quickly put my nose back in my book and pretend to be engrossed. He taps me on the shoulder and I look up.

"Here, Mahmah," he holds up the rain lilies to me with a proud smile. His freckles stand out on his face and he has drops of water on his nose.

"I got you some flowers and this stick."

My throat chokes and I feel my eyes begin to swim as I look down at my valiant little gentleman.

"Thank you, buddy," I say, "They're

beautiful."

"Here," he says, "Let's put them in a vase for all of us," and he hands me a dirt-covered Styrofoam coffee cup.

"I love you, Mahmah," he says, and leans his head against my cheek. I put my arms around his cold, skinny shoulders and wrap a blanket around him.

"You want to come sit on my lap?" I ask him, "I think I need to hold you."

He nods and climbs up and we huddle on the couch. I listen to his heart beating and nothing else matters to me in that moment.

* * * * *

And then there are those other days, those desolate days when everything is wrong and my foundations are shaking and I struggle to remember the good that exists around me. When dark, thick sadness threatens to overwhelm me and my soul is bruised.

That is when I pull out a memory like one of these. I hold it in my calloused hands and turn it over and over and hold it up to the light. I examine it from every angle and relive it again.

I remember once more the blessing of loving and being wildly loved by a little tribe whose antics are far too outlandish and sincere to be invented by a creative mind.

I see a man who is aware of my deep imperfections and loves me still.

I recall that there is a God in His heaven who holds me in the palm of His hand and understands me both when I am full of tears and when I am empty and poured out.

Then the ground levels out under my feet again and I stand still with my eyes closed and feel the wind blowing on my face. And I am content and grateful simply to be alive and breathing.

52027304R00138

Made in the USA
Charleston, SC
09 February 2016